HEALTH CARE IN TRANSITION

U.S. HEALTH CARE WORKFORCE: SUPPLY AND DEMAND PROJECTIONS AND FEDERAL PLANNING EFFORTS

HEALTH CARE IN TRANSITION

Additional books in this series can be found on Nova's website under the Series tab.

Additional e-books in this series can be found on Nova's website under the e-book tab.

HEALTH CARE IN TRANSITION

U.S. HEALTH CARE WORKFORCE: SUPPLY AND DEMAND PROJECTIONS AND FEDERAL PLANNING EFFORTS

SHELDON T. BARRETT
EDITOR

nova publishers
New York

Library of Congress Cataloging-in-Publication Data

ISBN: 978-1-63485-730-7

Published by Nova Science Publishers, Inc. † New York

CONTENTS

PREFACE

This book provides a review on the supply and demand projections and federal planning efforts in the U.S. health care workforce, which include primary care practitioners; non-primary care specialty and subspecialty clinicians; the nursing workforce; health support occupations; health technologist and technician occupations; pharmacists; occupational therapy and physical therapy; vision occupations; respiratory therapists; chiropractors and podiatrists; dieticians and nutritionists; and psychologists. Furthermore, this book examines the Department of Health and Human Service's (HHS) planning efforts for ensuring an adequate supply and distribution of the nation's health care workforce; the extent to which individual HHS health care workforce programs contribute to meeting national needs; and key components of the President's 2015 Budget which proposes major new investments to build the health care workforce and improve the delivery of health care services, particularly primary care services, across the nation.

In: U.S. Health Care Workforce
Editor: Sheldon T. Barrett
ISBN: 978-1-63485-730-7

Chapter 1

PROJECTING THE SUPPLY AND DEMAND FOR PRIMARY CARE PRACTITIONERS THROUGH 2020*

National Center for Health Workforce Analysis

LIST OF ACRONYMS

Acronym	Definition
AACN	American Association of Colleges of Nursing
AAMC	Association of American Medical Colleges
AAPA	American Academy of Physician Assistants
AMA	American Medical Association
BRFSS	Behavioral Risk Factor Surveillance System
CBO	Congressional Budget Office
CDC	Centers for Disease Control and Prevention
EHR	Electronic Health Record
FTE	Full-time equivalent
HIT	Health information technology
HPSA	Health Professional Shortage Area
HRSA	Health Resources and Services Administration

* This is an edited, reformatted and augmented version of a report issued by the U.S. Department of Health and Human Services, Health Resources and Services Administration, November 2013.

NAMCS	National Ambulatory Medical Care Survey
NCCPA	National Commission on Certification of Physician Assistants
NH	Non-Hispanic
NHAMCS	National Hospital Ambulatory Medical Care Survey
NIS	Nationwide Inpatient Sample
NP	Nurse Practitioner
NSSRN	National Sample Survey of Registered Nurses
PA	Physician Assistant
PCP	Primary Care Practitioner

I. Executive Summary

This study examines the adequacy of the future supply of primary care practitioners (PCPs) to meet the future demand for primary care services. Data on supply and demand for primary care services in 2010, with demand adjusted for physician shortages in Health Professional Shortage Areas (HPSAs), are used as a baseline to project supply and demand in 2020 for physicians, nurse practitioners (NPs), and physician assistants (PAs). The model assumes continuation of key trends in service utilization, practitioner practice patterns, and practitioner production. The model also accounts for aging and population growth and the expansion of coverage under the Affordable Care Act. The impact of the Affordable Care Act is modeled under the assumption that all states expand Medicaid. Therefore, the numbers reported here overestimate the demand for primary care services, until such time as all states fully implement the law. Projections of demand for each type of practitioner are based on how these practitioners are currently deployed to provide services.

Demand for primary care services is projected to increase through 2020, due largely to aging and population growth and, to a much lesser extent, the expanded insurance coverage implemented under the Affordable Care Act, which includes a number of investments that strengthen the primary care workforce. Consistent with prior studies, this analysis finds that demand for primary care physicians will grow more rapidly than the physician supply, resulting in a projected shortage of approximately 20,400 full-time equivalent (FTE) physicians.

The supply of NPs and PAs, however, is projected to grow rapidly and could mitigate the projected shortage of physicians if NPs and PAs continue to be effectively integrated into the primary care delivery system. In order for this integration to occur, patient and health system acceptance is necessary and the dissemination of more effective models of workforce deployment must continue. New models that allow for an increased role of NPs and PAs in the provision of primary care services, such as patient-centered medical homes that emphasize team-based care, have the potential to help address the projected shortage of primary care physicians.

Under a scenario assuming full deployment of available NPs and PAs, the projected shortage of PCPs in 2020 is only 6,400 FTEs. Physicians would remain the dominant provider of primary care services, decreasing from 77 percent of primary care services in 2010 to 72 percent in 2020.

A. Key Findings

Demand for primary care services is projected to grow, mostly due to population aging and growth.

- Aging and population growth are projected to account for 81 percent of the change in demand between 2010 and 2020.
- The remainder of the projected change in demand is associated with the estimated expansion of health insurance coverage under the full implementation of the Affordable Care Act, including an assumption that all states expand Medicaid.

Based on current utilization patterns, demand for primary care physicians is projected to grow more rapidly than physician supply.

- The number of primary care physicians is projected to increase from 205,000 FTEs in 2010 to 220,800 in 2020, an 8-percent increase.
- The total demand for primary care physicians is projected to grow by 28,700, from 212,500 FTEs in 2010 to 241,200 FTEs in 2020, a 14-percent increase.
- Without changes to how primary care is delivered, the growth in primary care physician supply will not be adequate to meet demand in 2020, with a projected shortage of 20,400 physicians. While this deficit is not as large as has been found in prior studies, the projected shortage of primary care physicians is still significant.

The primary care NP and PA workforces are projected to grow far more rapidly than the physician supply.

- The supply of primary care NPs is projected to increase by 30 percent, from 55,400 in 2010 to 72,100 in 2020. The supply of primary care PAs is projected to increase by 58 percent, from 27,700 to 43,900 over the same period.
- Assuming that NPs and PAs provide the same proportion of services in 2020 that they did in 2010, the combined demand for NPs and PAs would increase by only 17 percent. If NPs and PAs are used to provide a greater proportion of primary care services, their projected demand will be higher.

Increased use of NPs and PAs could somewhat alleviate the projected primary care physician shortage if they are effectively integrated into the health care delivery system.

- Under a scenario in which the rapidly growing NP and PA supply can effectively be integrated, the shortage of 20,400 physicians in 2020 could be reduced to 6,400 PCPs.
- If fully utilized, the percent of primary care services provided by NPs and PAs will grow from 23 percent in 2010 to 28 percent in 2020. Physicians would remain the dominant providers of primary care, only decreasing from 77 percent of the primary care services in 2010 to 72 percent in 2020.

B. Conclusion

The extent to which the national supply of PCPs will come close to meeting the national demand in 2020 will depend on a number of factors. Given the rapid growth in the NP and PA workforce, as well as ongoing efforts to effectively integrate these providers into the primary care delivery system, the projected physician shortage could be somewhat alleviated. Efficient use of NPs and PAs will require patient and health system acceptance and the continued dissemination of more effective models of workforce deployment. There are indications of the acceptance of these practitioners by patients.

The projections do not account for new programs and policies included in the Affordable Care Act. To help strengthen access to the primary care workforce, the Affordable Care Act invests in health workforce training, including: a $1.5 billion investment in the National Health Service Corps Scholarship and Loan Repayment programs over five years; a substantial expansion of Community Health Centers; and $230 million over five years to primarily train medical residents in community-based settings. The Affordable Care Act also includes incentives that encourage greater emphasis on initiatives (i.e., Primary Care Medical Homes and Accountable Care Organizations) which are anticipated to result in more effective use of providers in care delivery. Such programs and policies are designed to increase the supply of PCPs and increase the effectiveness of their use through models emphasizing team-based care. Such changes could further integrate NPs and PAs in the provision of primary care services and have the potential to somewhat alleviate the projected shortage of primary care physicians.

Finally, the national averages reported here mask substantial distributional disparities across the United States. It is anticipated that some communities will continue to face significant shortages. Ensuring patient access to primary care will continue to require programs and policies to address the maldistribution of the primary care workforce.

Given the importance of access to primary care for an effective health care system, the Health Resources and Services Administration (HRSA) will continue to monitor the supply and distribution of PCPs. HRSA also will periodically update these projections as new data and information become available.

C. Limitations of These Projections

Numerous factors will influence future supply and demand for PCPs. The baseline projections in this report do not account for new programs and policies that may help grow the supply of PCPs or reform the health care delivery system. However, these projections do consider the estimated impact of expanded health insurance coverage associated with full implementation of the Affordable Care Act.

Further, this study does not address provider shortages at subnational levels of geography. National projections represent the average adequacy of supply: some areas have a supply of PCPs well above the national norm or average; other areas have a supply that is inadequate to meet the need for PCPs. Geographic maldistribution of practitioners will mean some local areas will face practitioner shortages.

This study assumes that the supply and demand for PCPs was balanced in 2010 except for the number of physicians that would be needed to de-designate HPSAs. The HPSA shortfall is used as a proxy for the base-year national shortfall since it is the only federal measure of shortage available at this time. Shortages may exist in areas that are not designated as HPSAs or in professions not currently covered by HPSAs (such as NPs and PAs).

II. Introduction

The availability of primary care services is essential for an effective and efficient health care system. Having an adequate supply and distribution of well-prepared primary care practitioners (PCPs) will help ensure the availability of primary care services for the nation. This study was undertaken to assess whether the future supply of PCPs is likely to be sufficient to meet the future demand for primary care. In order to make this assessment, the study examines the projected supply of physicians, NPs, and PAs.

The national demand for primary care services can be defined as the quantity and mix of services that society is willing to pay for based on population needs, economic constraints such as income and prices, and technological considerations for what is possible to provide. It reflects the realities of the current health care system with its reimbursement structure, incentives and disincentives for health care use and delivery patterns, public expectations, and other personal and systematic economic considerations.

The demand for primary care practitioners is the number and mix of clinicians needed to meet the demand for services. Demand for practitioners in specific disciplines is influenced by practitioner productivity, scope of practice, and the structure and financing of the health care delivery system. A variety of configurations of PCPs can meet the demand for primary care services.

The development of a baseline for supply and demand is based upon recent patterns of use of services stratified by population characteristics, trends in the education and training of PCPs (where 2010 data are not available), and recent practice patterns of current PCPs. Using the typical projection model method, the study assumes that supply and demand are in balance in the base year (2010), except for the added demand for the number of primary care physicians needed to de-designate primary care HPSAs. From this baseline, the study considers a variety of potential changes in the future and their possible impact on both supply and demand. Some of these changes can be predicted with reasonable confidence, like the aging of the population. Others, such as changes in productivity, practice hours, and retirement patterns, are less certain.

The projections in this report take into consideration the estimated impact of expanded health insurance coverage associated with the full implementation of the Affordable Care Act, including an assumption that all states expand Medicaid. However, these projections do not account for new programs and policies that will help grow the supply of PCPs or reform the health care delivery system. Many provisions included in the Affordable Care Act, for example, broad implementation of patient-centered medical homes, are designed to implement change in the health care delivery system. The impact of such provisions, at this point, is difficult to quantify in a projection model. Thus, the projection model predicts future demand fundamentally on the utilization patterns in the delivery system of the recent past for which there are data.

National projections of supply and demand can assist policymakers and practitioners in assessing the adequacy of supply for the nation as a whole. National projections, however, do not reveal problems that exist in specific geographic areas, because they represent the average adequacy of supply across the nation. While some areas have a supply of PCPs well above the national average, other areas have a supply that is inadequate to meet the need for primary care services. Hence, the national projections in this report do not provide a complete picture of the adequacy of the supply of PCPs needed to ensure patient access to care. More detailed analysis of the adequacy of supply within local geographic areas—whether counties, cities, townships, or neighborhoods—is needed to fully understand the adequacy of the primary care workforce and how that workforce would need to be distributed across the nation to ensure access.

A. Definition of Primary Care

The Institute of Medicine's Committee on the Future of Primary Care defined primary care as: "The provision of integrated, accessible health services by clinicians who are accountable for addressing a large majority of personal health care needs, developing a sustained partnership with patients, and practicing in the context of family and community."[1] Medical specialties that could meet the criteria for a PCP include general and family medicine, general pediatrics, general internal medicine, and geriatrics. While the majority of the nation's hospitalists— practitioners who mainly provide care to hospitalized patients—are trained in primary care specialties, they are excluded from practitioner counts in this study because they are not engaged in activities that meet the definition of primary care.[2] Disciplines generally considered in the definition of PCPs may include physicians, NPs, and PAs who trained and practice in primary care specialties.

A broader definition of primary care capacity could consider primary care services provided by physicians in other specialties. Some examples include internal medicine subspecialists like cardiologists or endocrinologists with whom a patient may have a long-term relationship and who may be the primary source of care for a chronic condition. Obstetrician/gynecologists also provide some primary care services and may be the principal source of care for some women. Similarly, a certified nurse midwife may provide some primary care for women. While these practitioners provide important services, this study excludes primary care services provided by these specialists. On the other hand, many primary care physicians also provide some specialty services that are often provided by specialists. For this study, these services are implicitly included because it is not possible to estimate the proportion of time primary care physicians spend providing specialty services.

III. PRIMARY CARE PHYSICIAN SUPPLY

A. Overview of the Supply Model

The starting point for projecting future supply is the current supply (see Exhibit 1). Projecting forward from the baseline, a number of factors are taken into account. Each year, new physicians enter the workforce after completing the required education and training and after other physicians retire. In addition, clinicians in the workforce may change their level of activity (i.e., average hours worked) or their area of practice.

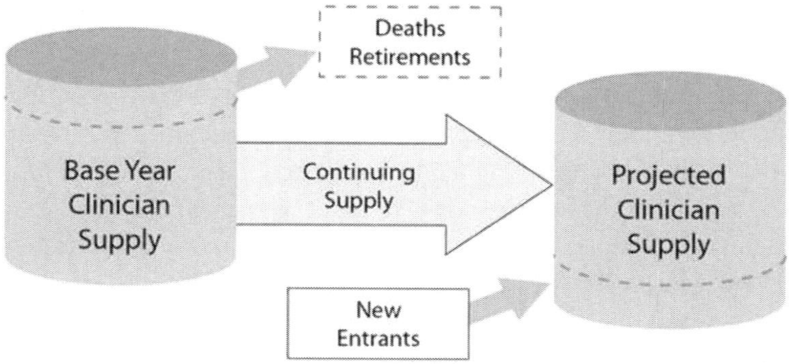

Exhibit 1. Projecting Primary Care Physician Supply.

Two measures commonly used to track clinician supply are: (1) the number of clinicians actively engaged in patient care activities (*active supply*) and (2) a measure that takes into account productivity (*FTE supply*). In this report, both supply and demand projections are calculated as FTEs rather than as persons or headcounts. For example, a clinician who works half the time of the typical physician counts as 0.5 FTE.

B. Estimating the Active Supply of Primary Care Physicians in 2010

Estimates of the number of primary care physicians engaged in patient care activities are based on data from multiple sources.[3] The American Medical Association (AMA) Masterfile, one of the most complete national sources of information on current physician supply, contains birth year, sex, self-reported primary specialty, primary activity (e.g., direct patient care, non-patient care, or resident), and other information. This source provides estimates of the number of active physicians by self-reported primary specialty, age, and sex.

There are limitations to the AMA Masterfile data. For example, there is a time lag between when a physician's activity status changes and when the information is updated in the Masterfile. The AMA updates the Masterfile using multiple sources, including licensure information, and attempts to contact about one-third of physicians each year. However, if physicians' status changes, there can be up to a three-year lag before their information in the Masterfile is corrected. Additionally, some physicians choose not to respond to AMA's request for information, which contributes further to the uncertainty of whether an individual physician is active or retired. The time lag in updating physicians' activity status creates the likelihood that the Masterfile overestimates the supply of active physicians—especially for older physicians.[4] This study excluded physicians age 75 and older listed as active in the AMA Masterfile, reflecting concerns about the accuracy of the AMA Masterfile regarding the activity status of older physicians.

In addition, comparison of physician self-reported activity status in the 2006 AMA Masterfile with the 2006 Association of American Medical Colleges (AAMC) survey of physicians from 50 to 74 years old suggests that activity status in the Masterfile for some of these physicians may be incorrect. Some physicians in this age group listed as active in the Masterfile reported in the AAMC survey that they are currently inactive, and vice versa.[5] The Masterfile lists as active only physicians working more than 20 hours per week in professional activities. The AAMC survey collected hours worked data on physicians working fewer than 20 hours. This study used an algorithm to adjust the estimated number of active physicians in the 2010 Masterfile. Using logistic regression analysis with activity status from the AAMC survey as the dependent variable, the analysis determined the probability that each physician age 51 to 74 in the Masterfile is active based on age, sex, specialty, and activity status in the Masterfile. Application of this retirement algorithm removes from the Masterfile active physician count approximately 20,000 physicians primarily engaged in patient care activities. The algorithm also adds to the count 17,000 physicians listed as "semi-retired" or "retired" (which includes those working fewer than 20 hours per week in professional activities).[6]

Estimates from the Robert Graham Center are that approximately 10,500 primary care physicians whose status is "unclassified" in the 2010 Masterfile are likely active in patient care. This analysis used estimates of primary care consistent with the Robert Graham Center's supply estimates, and it includes these unclassified physicians in the primary care category.[7]

The analysis classifies physician specialty based on self-reported primary specialty. Physicians without a reported specialty are proportionally reallocated across the other specialties based on the specialty distribution within their age, gender, and education type. The AMA Masterfile only recently added the specialty of "hospitalist" to its survey of physicians, and very few physicians self-reported as hospitalists. The Society of Hospital Medicine estimates that among the 28,000 hospitalists in practice in 2010, 82.3 percent are trained in general internal medicine, 6.5 percent in general pediatrics, 4.0 percent in an internal medicine subspecialty, 3.7 percent in family practice, 3.1 percent in general pediatrics, and 0.4 percent in a pediatrics subspecialty.[8] Estimates of the specialty distribution for hospitalists, as reported by the Society of Hospital Medicine, were used to remove hospitalists from the primary care supply estimates.

Finally, estimates of practicing primary care physicians from sample surveys of physicians, in particular the National Ambulatory Medical Care Survey (NAMCS) and the Health Tracking Physician Survey,[9] suggest that there may be fewer primary care physicians. That is, additional physicians classified as active in the Masterfile may be either inactive or no longer practicing in primary care settings. For example, during the data collection for the NAMCS and the Health Tracking Physician Survey, a greater proportion of physicians were found to be inactive (e.g., retired or deceased) than from initial adjustments to the AMA Masterfile. Others have used findings from the NAMCS, for example, to adjust estimates from the AMA Masterfile downward.[10] The NAMCS is an ongoing annual survey that uses the AMA Masterfile for its sampling frame. Based primarily upon review of this survey, the study reduces the preliminary estimate from the AMA Masterfile by 8 percent to account for additional inactive and non-primary care physicians.[11]

After all adjustments were made, the study estimates that there were 205,000 practicing primary care physicians in 2010. Of these, 91,300 are in family practice, 65,600 in general internal medicine, 44,800 in pediatrics, and 3,300 in geriatrics.

C. Projecting the Future Supply of Primary Care Physicians

The main drivers of the future number of active practitioners are the number of newly trained practitioners entering the workforce (entrants) and the number of practitioners leaving the workforce because of retirement, disability, or death (attrition). The projection also adjusted for changes over time in physician characteristics that are associated with patient care hours worked per week.

1. Entrants

Training new practitioners is a vital component of maintaining an adequate long-term supply of health professionals. This study projects supply using best estimates of the number of new primary care physicians who will be trained between 2010 and 2020, given current plans by educational institutions to expand education and training capacity.[12]

In order to become a physician licensed to practice medicine in the United States, some accredited graduate medical education is required. Physicians enter graduate medical education through one of three routes: graduation from a U.S. school of allopathic medicine (i.e., U.S.-trained Medical Doctors), graduation from a U.S. school of osteopathic medicine (i.e., Doctors of Osteopathic Medicine), or graduation from an international medical school (i.e., International Medical Graduates).

The number of physicians beginning their graduate medical education in the United States in 2010 was approximately 26,000—up from around 24,000 in 2004.[13] Using graduate medical education completion data published from the AMA and American Osteopathic Association statistics, the study calculates that the nation produces approximately 8,700 primary care physicians annually, with the number projected to rise slightly each year over the next decade.[14,15]

The distribution of sex and specialty choice of new entrants to the physician workforce is modeled using recently published data for Accreditation Council for Graduate Medical Education programs.[16] The age distribution of physicians completing medical school in 2009 comes from the Medical School Graduation Questionnaire: 2013 All Schools Summary Report.[17] When the age distribution of physicians completing graduate medical education is calculated (see Exhibit 2), the study adds the average post-graduate training (residency/fellowship) duration to the age distribution. This simplifying assumption may misrepresent the actual age distribution of new physicians for some specialties to the extent that older medical school graduates, for example, are more likely to choose a specialty with a shorter residency.

2. Retention

In some medical specialties, a relatively large proportion of physicians are approaching traditional retirement age. The 2006 AAMC Survey of Physicians Over Age 50 collected information on age of retirement (if retired) or age expecting to retire (if still active). Historical retirement rates and expected retirement rates by physician age, sex, and medical specialty are calculated using these data. These rates are combined with data on mortality rates for men and women in the United States obtained from the Centers for Disease Control and Prevention (CDC). The mortality rates take into consideration that people in professional occupations tend to have lower mortality rates through age 65, as compared with national mortality rates.[18] Age-adjusted mortality rates for White males in professional and technical occupations are approximately 25 percent lower than national rates; for White females, the mortality rates for professional and technical occupations are 15 percent lower than overall rates.

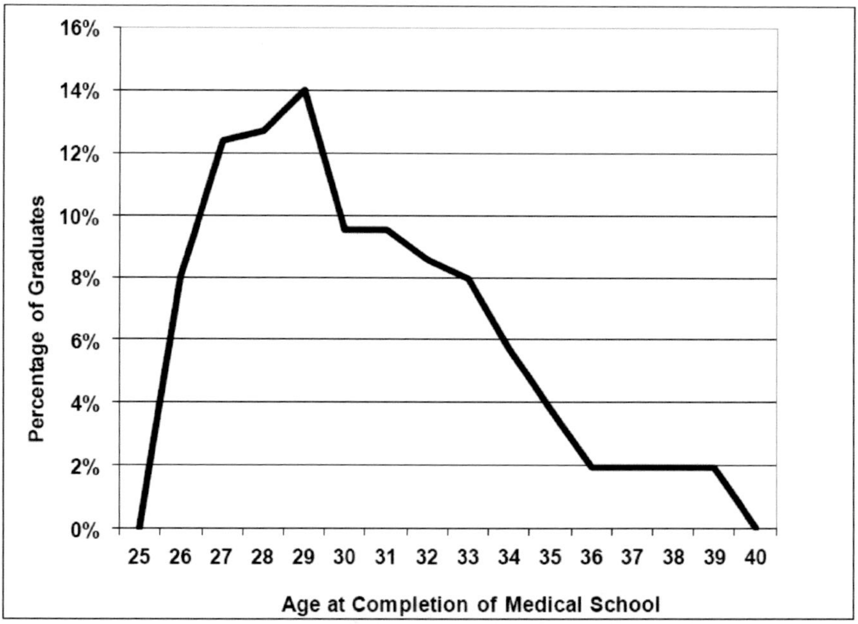

Data Source: AAMC Medical School Graduation Questionnaire: 2013 All Schools Summary Report.

Exhibit 2. Physician Age Distribution at Completion of Medical School, 2009.

3. Projected Changes in Patient Care Hours Worked

The study adjusts average hours worked for changes over time in the distribution of physician age and sex, because these characteristics are associated with the average patient care hours worked per week. Average hours tend to be lower for women than for men, especially during child-rearing ages. While hours worked by male physicians start to decline in the late 50s, the decline for women, on average, starts in the early 60s.

Physician-level data on patient care hours worked per week comes from two sources: (1) the 2006 AAMC Survey of Physicians Over Age 50, which provided information for approximately 9,000 respondents, and (2) a survey sponsored by HRSA during 2002 and 2003, which collected information for approximately 46,800 physicians. The AAMC survey data are used for the specialties in which the AAMC oversampled physicians and for physicians older than age 50. For all other specialties and for physicians younger than age 50, the study uses data from the HRSA-sponsored survey. Data are unavailable for geriatric medicine, so the study assumes that patterns of hours worked in geriatric medicine are similar to patterns for general internal medicine.

Dividing average hours worked by practitioners of a given age and sex by the average hours worked in that profession provides an estimate of the average FTE by demographic group. When general internists are used as an example, the patient care hours in the profession average about 45 hours per week (see Exhibit 3). Men age 50 to 54 work, on average, 53 patient care hours per week (or approximately 18 percent higher than the overall average of 45), while men age 70 to 74 who are still working average 34 patient care hours per week (or 75 percent of the average). Therefore, when FTEs for general internal medicine are calculated in this example, the study counts each male physician age 50 to 54 as 1.18 FTE and each male physician age 70 to 74 as 0.75 FTE. This approach adjusts the FTE count over time as the demographic composition of the health workforce changes.

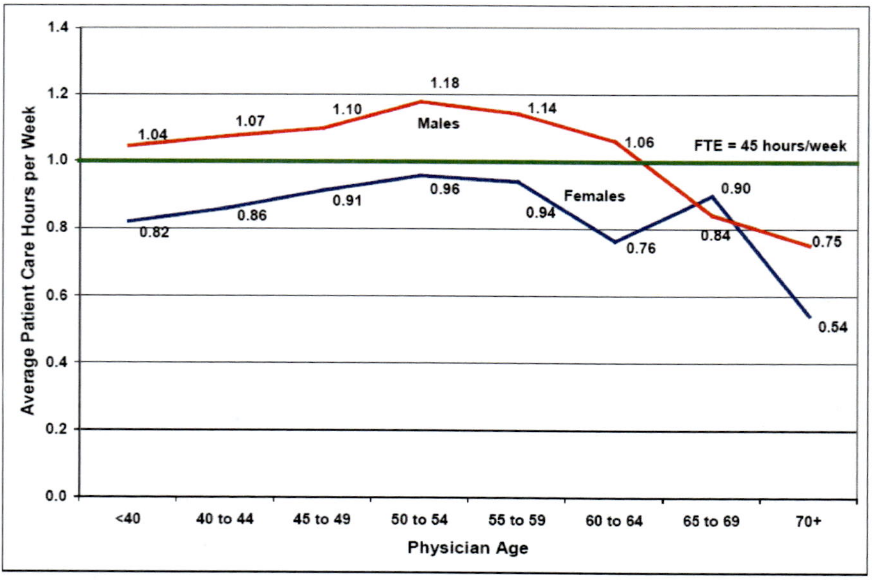

Data Sources: Analysis of HRSA 2002-2003 Survey and AAMC 2006 Survey of Physicians Over Age 50.

Exhibit 3. Average Patient Care Hours Worked per Week: General Internal Medicine.

D. Projected Change in Primary Care Physician Supply, 2010 Through 2020

The final projection is that there will be 220,800 FTE primary care physicians in 2020, an increase from 205,000 FTEs in 2010. This is an absolute increase of 15,800 FTE and is an 8-percent increase in overall supply.

IV. NP SUPPLY

A. Estimating the Active Supply of NPs in 2010

Approximately 55,400 NPs were clinically active in primary care in 2010. Estimates were derived from analysis and comparison of data from multiple sources, because there is no single comprehensive source of data on NPs. Estimates of clinically active NPs and the proportion practicing in primary care generated using the 2008 National Sample Survey of Registered Nurses (NSSRN) were similar to those recently reported by the Agency for Healthcare Research and Quality.[19] Based on the 2008 NSSRN, projected forward to 2010, it is estimated that there were approximately 110,800 clinically active NPs, of which half (55,400) were practicing in primary care.

B. Projecting the Future Supply of NPs

According to the American Association of Colleges of Nursing (AACN), more than 11,100 NPs graduated at the master's or post-master's level in academic year 2009 to 2010. This number increased to more than 14,400 in 2012.[20] Moreover, the number of NP graduates has increased steadily over the past eight years and more than doubled between 2002 and 2012 (see Exhibit 4). An analysis performed by HRSA's National Center for Health Workforce Analysis (the National Center) suggests that a portion of newly trained NPs may not practice in the NP role, instead serving in registered nursing positions not requiring NP training. The current study projects a moderation of the recent rapid growth. It further estimates that 50 percent of these NPs will practice in primary care specialties.[21]

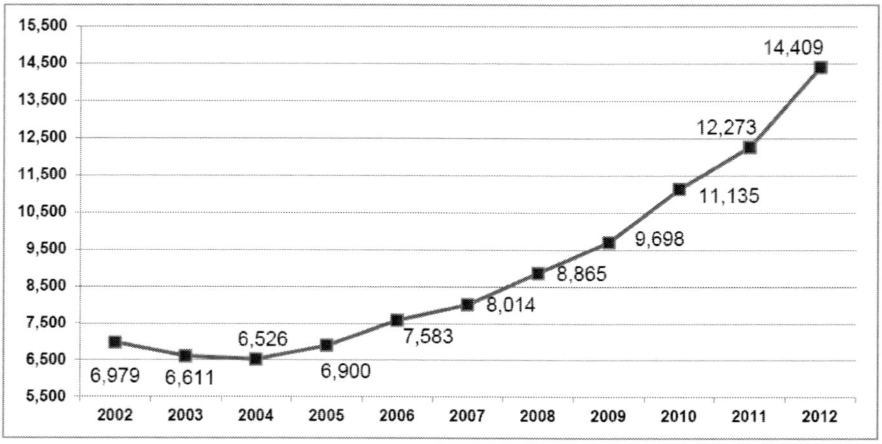

Data Source: HRSA compilation of data from the AACN Annual Survey (in collaboration with the National Organization of Nurse Practitioner Faculties for collection of nurse practitioner data). Note: Counts include master's and post-master's degree NP and NP/clinical nurse specialist graduates as well as bachelor's-todoctorate of nursing practice graduates.

Exhibit 4. Annual Number of Graduates From NP Programs: Master's and Post-Master's Graduates, 2002 Through 2012.

In total, the supply of NPs delivering primary care is projected to increase by 30 percent, from 55,400 in 2010 to 72,100 in 2020. This is an increase of 16,700 practitioners.

V. PA SUPPLY

A. Estimating the Active Supply of PAs in 2010

There were an estimated 27,700 PAs clinically active in primary care in 2010. This estimate is based on the 2008 American Academy of Physician Assistants (AAPA) Physician Assistant Census. It is projected forward to 2010 based on the addition of approximately 12,000 new graduates over the two years and the subtraction of 3 percent of PAs annually for expected attrition. Of the 84,000 PAs the current study estimates as clinically active in 2010, approximately one-third (27,700) are in primary care, and two-thirds (56,300) are in non-primary care specialties.

B. Projecting the Future Supply of PAs

The projection assumes that the number of new PA graduates will increase by 200 annually, from approximately 6,000 in 2010 to 8,000 by 2020.[22] The number of accredited PA programs has steadily risen over the past decade from 134 in 2003 to 173 in 2013, with anticipated additional growth in the near future.[23] The number of certified PAs has also risen over the past decade (see Exhibit 5). Approximately one-third of new PA graduates are assumed to enter a primary care specialty.[24]

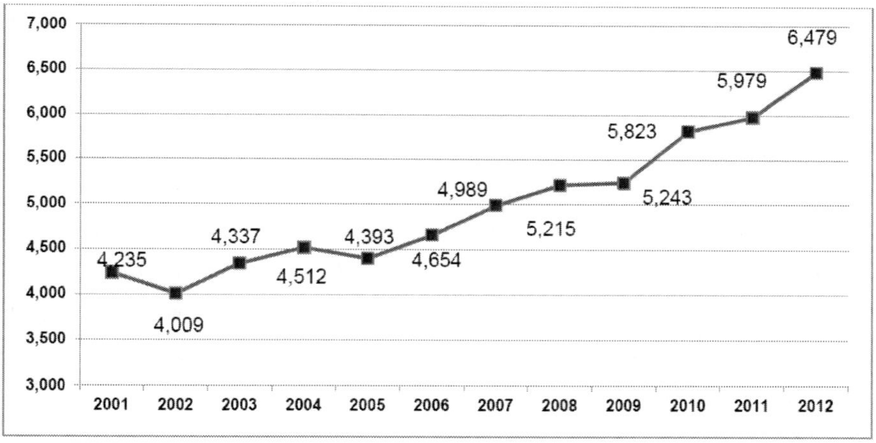

Data Source: National Commission on Certification of Physician Assistants (NCCPA), "Certified Physician Assistant Population Trends"; 2012 data from personal communication with NCCPA, January 16, 2013.

Exhibit 5. Annual Number of Newly Certified PAs, 2001 Through 2012.

Taking new graduates into account, the supply of PAs delivering primary care is projected to increase by 58 percent, from 27,700 in 2010 to 43,900 in 2020.

VI. Primary Care Demand

A. Background

The national demand for primary care services can be defined as the quantity and mix of services that society is willing to pay for based on population needs, economic constraints such as income and prices, and technological considerations of what is possible to provide. The demand for *primary care practitioners* (PCPs) is the number and mix of clinicians needed to meet the demand for services. Therefore, practitioner productivity, scope of practice, and how the health care system is structured for care delivery influence the demand for practitioners in specific disciplines. In reality, different configurations and mixes of PCPs can meet demand for primary care services. This study projects future demand for *primary care services* using the current utilization patterns and rates by population characteristic. Those estimates are then used to project the demand for PCPs. Both the demand for services and the resulting demand for practitioners are influenced by the complex interaction of the following determinants:

- **Population needs** are highly correlated with demographics such as the size and age of the population and the prevalence of chronic conditions. Projected increases in population, especially growth in the older population, portends strong growth in demand for primary care services for adults. Geographic variation and trends over time in chronic diseases and risk factors (e.g., obesity) affect the need for primary care services.
- **Economic constraints and prices** affect the ability and willingness of consumers to pay for services and influence how the health care system evolves to provide such services. Expanded health insurance coverage that will occur because of the Affordable Care Act is anticipated to increase demand for primary care services by reducing financial barriers to accessing care.
- **Technological and medical innovations** influence the services provided and care delivery. Since many medical advances improve survival and lifestyle for those with chronic illness, demand will likely increase. At the same time, advances in technology could increase practitioner productivity, requiring fewer practitioners to care for a given population.
- **System-induced demand** is the portion of health care use generated by health care practitioners that includes practitioner referrals for tests, procedures, and follow-up visits.[25]
- **Public perceptions and expectations** regarding appropriate use of health care services and the ability of health care to improve health influence the public's demand for services.

B. Estimate of PCP Demand in 2010

The typical projections methodology used in this study assumes supply equals demand in the base year. This methodology was modified to account for unmet need in primary care HPSAs. It is estimated that there were 205,000 primary care physicians in 2010. The estimated shortfall of 7,500 primary care physicians needed to de-designate primary care HPSAs was added,[26] yielding a demand of 212,500 physicians in 2010. The current shortfall is assumed to be for general practice, family medicine, and general internal medicine.[27,28]

Consistent with the projections methodology, the supply of NPs and PAs in 2010 is assumed to be equal to the demand for these practitioners. Therefore, 2010 demand for NPs is set at 55,400 and 27,700 for PAs.

C. Estimating Demand in 2020

Drivers of the projected demand for primary care services in 2020 include population growth and associated demographic changes. Drivers also include the expanded health insurance coverage that will result from the implementation of the Affordable Care Act in 2014. Before projections of future demand, a number of analyses were performed to understand the components of demand for primary care services in the base year.

1. Baseline Patterns of Health Care Use

i. Data Sources

Current patterns of health care use and delivery provide a starting point for understanding demand for primary care services. Using national data sources, the study estimates the proportion of primary care clinician time spent providing care to different subsets of the population in different health care delivery settings: (1) visits to practitioner offices and community health centers; (2) visits to hospital/clinic outpatient, emergency departments; and (3) hospital rounds. A small portion of care is provided in other settings (e.g., nursing homes and home health).

Data sources for analyzing encounter rates by patient characteristics include the 2005 to 2007 NAMCS, 2005 to 2007 National Hospital Ambulatory Medical Care Survey (NHAMCS), and 2007 Nationwide Inpatient Sample (NIS).[29] Rather than focusing on total encounters, the analysis estimated the proportion of office-based services provided to each population defined by seven age groups, sex, four race/ethnicity groups, and three insurance categories.[30] This usage information, combined with estimates of the number of FTE primary care clinicians providing office-based care (discussed later), forms the basis for constructing national practitioner-to-population ratios.

Many physicians trained in primary care participate in patient care activities outside of office visits—such as hospital rounds and ambulatory visits in clinics, hospital outpatient clinics, emergency departments, and urgent care centers. The analysis utilizes patient diagnosis codes and demographics found in the NIS (used to model hospital inpatient care) and the NHAMCS (used to model hospital outpatient and emergency care) for its estimates. With these data, the analysis estimates the patients most likely to be seen in the hospital by a family practitioner or general internist, a pediatrician, or a geriatrician. This information, in combination with estimates of the portion of physician time spent in hospital rounds and hospital outpatient or emergency departments, informed the estimates of practitioner-topopulation ratios for inpatient care and for outpatient/emergency-based care.

Information from the following sources contributed to the estimate of the average proportion of time physicians spend providing care in different settings:

- The Medical Group Management Association's Physician Compensation and Production Survey (2009 report based on 2008 data), which contains information on average volume of services provided in each setting;
- The American Board of Internal Medicine's Practice Characteristics Survey combined across multiple years, which provides estimates of the proportion of physician time engaged in different care activities; and
- AMA's 2003 Physician Socioeconomic Statistics, which provides estimates of the amount of time and services provided in different care delivery settings.

ii. Practitioner-to-Population Ratios

Estimates of FTE practitioners per 100,000 persons in each age group (see Exhibit 6) produce the practitioner-to-population ratio estimates. These ratios reflect: (1) patient encounters and physician time across different settings of care (based upon analysis of the multiple data sources outlined above); and (2) how the current primary care workload is distributed across patients (by age) and primary care discipline. At the national level, there are an estimated 98 FTE PCPs actively engaged in patient care per 100,000 population. Aggregate estimates range from a low of 41 FTE practitioners per 100,000 persons age 18 to 20 years to a high of 194 FTEs per 100,000 persons age zero to 5 years.

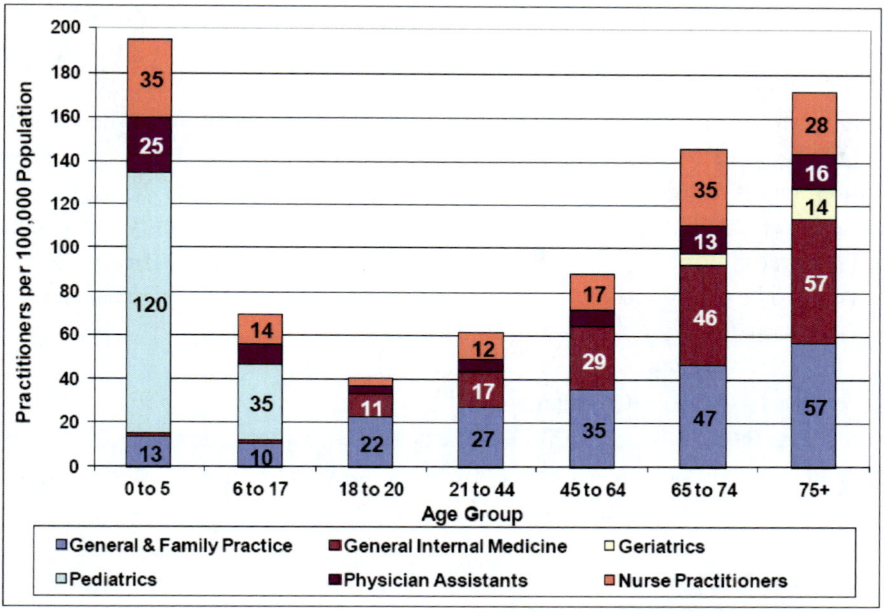

Data Source: Analysis of the multiple sources of data outlined in this report on patient utilization by setting (e.g., the NAMCS, NHAMCS, and NIS) and those on physician time allocation across settings of care.

Exhibit 6. Estimated Use of PCPs (FTEs) per 100,000 Persons Within Each Age Group, 2010.

2. Key Determinants of Future Demand

To estimate future demand for primary care services, national practitioner-to-population ratios to the projected future population are applied—adjusting for demographics, obesity rates, and insurance coverage (including the anticipated expansion of health insurance coverage due to the passage of the Affordable Care Act[31]). This section discusses these key demand determinants and trends.

i. Population Aging and Growth

Projections of the population developed by the U.S. Census Bureau for 2008 through 2050 (based on the 2000 Census and released in 2008) for age, sex, and race/ethnicity informed the study projections. U.S. Census Bureau projections suggest that the overall U.S. population will grow by approximately 10 percent over the next decade. However, the projected growth rate is much higher for the populations age 65 to 74 (50-percent growth) and age 75 and older (20 percent). The growth rate is lower for the age group zero to 17 (9 percent) and the age 18 to 64 population (5 percent). Since the amount of primary care services sought by patients varies substantially by age, these demographics suggest a growing demand for geriatrics. The demographics also suggest that a greater percentage of the patients seen by family physicians and general internists will be older individuals who require significantly more services. The study makes similar projections of demand for primary care services stratified by sex and race/ethnicity.[32]

ii. Health Insurance Coverage

Using the 2007 and 2008 American Community Survey,[33] the study estimates the proportion of the population uninsured in each demographic group. Applying these rates to the 2010 population suggests that 44.5 million people lack insurance coverage.

The Affordable Care Act extends coverage to many uninsured individuals beginning in 2014. The Congressional Budget Office (CBO) estimated that 8 percent of the U.S. population younger than 65 years of age would remain uninsured after implementation of the Affordable Care Act, assuming complete Medicaid expansion across U.S. states.[34] In order to model the implications of the Affordable Care Act, the study uses estimates of the proportion uninsured in each demographic who are non-citizens as a proxy for undocumented immigrants who may remain uninsured. The study also scales the proportion of citizens remaining uninsured in each demographic based upon the CBO estimate of 8-percent uninsured among the population younger than 65.

For modeling primary care demand, the study assumes that newly insured individuals will take on the health care use patterns of the commercially insured population within their demographic. Therefore, the anticipated increase in demand for primary care services reflects the difference between patterns for the commercially insured and patterns for the uninsured, controlling for age, sex, and race/ethnicity.

It is important to note that the demand for primary care services will likely also change because of other provisions included in the Affordable Care Act, such as changes in reimbursement rates and practice design. However, there is insufficient information to quantify the effect of these changes.

iii. Disease Risk Factors: Obesity Rates

The demand projections reflect variation in obesity rates and their implications for use of primary care services. Although a number of disease risk factors influence the demand for primary care services, available data and modeling techniques limited the number of risk factors that could be incorporated into this study. Obesity was selected for use because of its correlation with multiple diseases, including heart disease, stroke, and type 2 diabetes, as well as its increasing prevalence over the past few decades.[35] The study relies on survey findings from the Behavioral Risk Factor Surveillance System (BRFSS), which is fielded by CDC, and captures information on obesity and other health characteristics of a representative sample of adults throughout the United States. In order to increase the sample size, two years (2007 and 2008) of data were combined.[36] Because of small sample size in some demographic groups, to estimate obesity rates, logistic regression was used, with each individual in BRFSS as the unit of observation. The dependent variable is whether the person is obese (yes=1, no=0). The explanatory variables include dichotomous variables (yes=1, no=0) for age group, sex, race/ethnicity group, and state of residence.[37]

Obesity rates vary significantly by age, sex, and race/ethnicity. As reported by CDC and reflected in this analysis, compared with White adults, obesity rates for African Americans/Blacks are 36 percent higher, and rates for Hispanics are nearly 20 percent higher.[38] Trends in obesity rates suggest that the rate of growth has slowed substantially.[39] For modeling demand, it is assumed that obesity rates within each demographic group will remain constant over time. Hence, changes in demand over time associated with obesity in the modeling of demand are driven by the overall obesity rate produced by changes in the population demographic composition.

D. Results: Drivers of Projected Future Demand for Primary Care Services

Changing demographics of the population, including the aging and growth of the population, account for the majority (81 percent) of the projected increase in demand for PCPs between 2010 and 2020. In contrast, only 19 percent of the increased demand for PCPs from 2010 through 2020 is associated with the estimated expansion of the population covered by health insurance with the full implementation of the Affordable Care Act. If all states do not expand Medicaid, the percent of demand due to coverage expansion will be even less. This finding is consistent with several recent studies that have estimated the increased demand for primary care resulting from coverage expansions under the Affordable Care Act at 2 to 3 percent.[40]

VII. Projected Adequacy of Future Supply of PCPs

The study applies the national practitioner-to-population ratios for each demographic and insurance category to the projected future population. Then, the study translates projected demand for primary care services to projected demand for primary care practitioners, assuming continuation of current utilization patterns of physicians, NPs, and PAs.

A. Physicians

Between 2010 and 2020, the estimated total supply of primary care physicians grows more slowly than the levels needed to meet projected demand for health care services from physicians. The number of primary care physicians is projected to increase from 205,000 FTEs in 2010 to 220,800 in 2020, an 8-percent increase. However, the total demand for primary care physicians is projected to grow by 28,700, from 212,500 FTEs in 2010 to 241,200 FTEs in 2020, a 14-percent increase (see Exhibit 7). Without changes such as how primary care is delivered, the growth in primary care physician supply will not be adequate to meet demand in 2020, with a projected shortage of 20,400 physicians.

B. NPs and PAs

The supply of primary care NPs and PAs is estimated to grow faster than the levels required to meet demand if the current physician-to-NP/PA ratios in care delivery are maintained (see Exhibit 8). From 2010 through 2020, the supply of primary care NPs is projected to increase by 30 percent and the supply of primary care PAs is projected to increase by 58 percent. Assuming that NPs and PAs provide the same proportion of services in 2020 that they did in 2010, the combined demand for NPs and PAs would increase by only 17 percent. However, if NPs and PAs provide a greater share of primary care services, their effective demand would be higher.

	2010	**2020**
Total primary care physician demand (FTE)	212,500[a]	241,200[c]
General[b]	164,400	187,300
Pediatrics	44,800	49,600
Geriatrics	3,300	4,300
Primary care physician supply	205,000	220,800
Supply and demand	(7,500)	(20,400)

[a] National demand projections presented in this report assume that in 2010 the national supply of primary care physicians was adequate except for the approximately 7,500 FTEs needed to de-designate the primary care HPSAs.

[b]This category includes general and family practice, and general internal medicine. [c] Assumes all states expand Medicaid.

Exhibit 7. Projected Demand for Primary Care Physicians.

Provider Type/Specialty	2010	2020
Supply		
Nurse Practitioners	55,400	72,100
Physician Assistants	27,700	43,900
Demand		
Nurse Practitioners	55,400	64,700
Physician Assistants	27,700	32,700
Supply and Demand		
Nurse Practitioners	*	7,400
Physician Assistants	*	11,200

*There were no data available for estimating if there were base year shortages of NPs and PAs. Note: Counts of NPs and PAs are not adjusted for productivity.

Exhibit 8. Projected Supply and Demand for Primary Care NPs and Pas.

VIII. Discussion

At the national level, both the supply of and demand for PCPs will grow over the next decade. The growth in primary care physician supply alone will not be adequate to meet demand in 2020 under current configurations of care provisions. Given the projected growth in the NP and PA workforce, as well as ongoing efforts to effectively integrate these providers into the primary care delivery system, the projected physician shortage could be somewhat alleviated. Efficient use of NPs and PAs will require patient and health system acceptance and the continued dissemination of more effective models of workforce deployment. There are indications of the acceptance of these practitioners by patients.

NPs and PAs are not substitutes for physicians, but they have an important role in the health care system and are trained to provide some of the same services as physicians. Additionally, since NPs and PAs do not provide the same volume of services as physicians, projections of the extent to which NPs and PAs could help alleviate the physician shortage are dependent upon productivity assumptions.

Applying a 0.75 weighting to NPs and PAs relative to primary care physicians could help estimate the potential impact NPs and PAs could have on alleviating the primary care physician shortage. This weighting reflects the consensus of the Negotiated Rulemaking Committee on the Designation of Medically Underserved Populations and Health Professional Shortage Areas.[41]

Under a scenario in which the rapidly growing NP and PA supply can be effectively integrated, and using a 0.75 FTE weight, the shortage of 20,400 physicians in 2020 could be reduced to 6,400 PCPs. Physicians would still remain the dominant providers of primary care, decreasing from 77 percent of the primary care services in 2010 to 72 percent in 2020, but the percent of primary care services provided by NPs and PAs would grow from 23 percent in 2010 to 28 percent in 2020.

Such offset assumes a reorganization of primary care in which NPs and PAs deliver a greater proportion of the services than they do within the present system. It also anticipates, to some extent, a redesign of service delivery in physician practices whereby NPs and PAs provide a greater share of primary care services than they do now, to complement the services provided by physicians.

Improving the efficiency of health care service delivery through team-based models of care will help increase access to services. In 2009, the AAMC conducted a survey of primary care physicians and asked the physicians what steps they would take if their practice experienced a significant increase in demand, such as from the Affordable Care Act. Preliminary findings suggest that many practices would likely respond to increases in demand for services by hiring additional support staff (52.7 percent), physicians (46.5 percent), NPs (43.7 percent), and PAs (33.6 percent).[42] When asked what they thought society should do to expand primary care capacity, these same physicians responded that various health care system redesign initiatives would have an impact. The most common response was to increase the efficiency of care delivery by reducing paperwork (90-percent response), improving productivity (69 percent), and providing technology (66 percent).

Increasing the efficiency of care delivery through greater reliance on technology and reducing non-direct care activities (such as paperwork) may also have the potential to improve adequacy of primary care supply. Blanchfield et al. reported that as much as four hours per week of physician time that is spent on paperwork could be directed to other activities if the health care system streamlined clinical service billing processes.[43] These four hours per week, if redirected to patient care activities, would be equivalent to increasing primary care supply by approximately 11 percent. These efficiency gains would help close the gap between supply and demand.

Some medical and technological advances have the potential to increase practitioner productivity. For example, the Health Information Technology for Economic and Clinical Health Act, which defines and encourages "meaningful use" of Electronic Health Records (EHRs). EHRs allow practitioners to more efficiently manage patient care, thus reducing demand. In large part because of increased funding for health information technology (HIT), the proportion of primary care physicians using EHRs doubled (from 20 to 39 percent) between 2009 and 2011.[44] HIT also exists in the form of decision support systems that facilitate diagnosis and allow practitioners to print customized information to help patients understand and manage their conditions, thereby saving the practitioner time. Finally, alternative communication methods (e.g., email and telephone) can allow practitioners greater flexibility in communicating with patients and reduce the need for face-to-face visits.

The experience over the past decade is encouraging in terms of the ability of the delivery system to make use of a growing supply of PAs and NPs. For example, the number of new PA graduates grew from 4,400 in 2000 to about 6,000 in 2010.[45] Despite this 36-percent increase, new PAs do not appear to be having any difficulty finding jobs. A recent study also found strong acceptance of care by PAs and NPs, especially by those who had previous direct experience with these practitioners.[46]

A. Geographic Disparities Will Likely Continue

Even with the potential for greater reliance on NPs and PAs to provide primary care services to patients, disparities will continue. National projections mask problems that exist in specific geographic areas. Some areas enjoy the benefit of a supply of PCPs well above the national average. Other areas have a supply that is inadequate to meet the need for primary care services. More detailed analysis of the adequacy of supply within local geographic areas— whether counties, cities, townships, or neighborhoods—is needed to better understand the adequacy of the primary care workforce and how the primary care workforce would need to be distributed across the nation to ensure access.

Ensuring access to primary care for all Americans will continue to require programs and policies to address the maldistribution of the primary care workforce. Given the importance of access to primary care for an effective health care system, HRSA will continue to monitor the supply and distribution of PCPs. HRSA also will periodically update these projections as new data and information become available.

B. Limitations of These Projections

Numerous factors will influence future supply and demand for PCPs. The projections in this report do not account for new programs and policies that may help grow the supply of PCPs or reform the health care delivery system. While the projections do consider the estimated impact of expanded health insurance coverage associated with full implementation of the Affordable Care Act, if all states do not expand Medicaid, the numbers in this report are likely an overestimate.

A number of new programs and policies included in the Affordable Care Act are designed to increase the supply of PCPs and increase the effectiveness of their use through models emphasizing team-based care, such as patient-centered medical homes. Such changes could allow for an increased role of NPs and PAs in the provision of primary care services and have the potential to help address the projected shortage of primary care physicians.

This study assumes that the supply and demand for PCPs was balanced in 2010 except for the number of physicians that would be needed to de-designate HPSAs. The HPSA shortfall is used as a proxy for the base-year national shortfall since it is the only federal measure of shortage currently available. Shortages may exist in areas that are not designated as HPSAs or in professions not currently covered by HPSAs (such as NPs and PAs).

Finally, while it is reasonable to use historical patterns to project future supply and demand, it is important to be aware that small changes in the parameters in the projections (such as changes in hours worked or retirement patterns) could have a notable effect on future supply and/or demand.

End Notes

[1] Donaldson, M. S., Yordy, K. D., Lohr, K. N. and Vanselow, N. A. (Eds.); Institute of Medicine, Division of Health Care Services, Committee on the Future of Primary Care. (1996). *Primary care: America's health in a new era.* Washington, DC: National Academy Press. Available online at: www.nap.edu/catalog.php?record_id=5152.

[2] Society of Hospital Medicine. (2010, June). 2010 Society of Hospital Medicine media kit. Available online at: www.hospitalmedicine.org/AM/Template.cfm?Section=Home&CONTENTID=23077&TEMPLATE=/CM/ContentD isplay.cfm.

[3] Estimates were developed in collaboration with the Agency for Healthcare Research and Quality, the Office of the Assistant Secretary for Planning and Evaluation, and the Robert Graham Center, from January through March 2011.

[4] Staiger, D. O., Auerbach, D. I. and Buerhaus, P. I. (2009). Comparison of physician workforce estimates and supply projections. *Journal of the American Medical Association*, *302*(15), 1674–1680.

[5] Jewett, E. A., Brotherton, S. E. and Ruch-Ross, H. (2011). A national survey of "inactive" physicians in the United States of America: Enticements to reentry. *Human Resources for Health*, *9*(7).

[6] The appendix of the following report outlines additional detail on applying this type of retirement algorithm: Dill, M. J. and Salsberg, E. S. (2008). *The complexities of physician supply and demand: Projections through 2025.* Washington, DC: Association of American Medical Colleges, Center for Workforce Studies.

[7] Personal communication with Stephen Pettersen and Robert Phillips at the Robert Graham Center on analysis conducted by the Robert Graham Center regarding the application of the AMA Masterfile to estimation of primary care physician counts. For more information about the Robert Graham Center, see www.grahamcenter.org/online/graham/home.html.

[8] Society of Hospital Medicine. (2010, June). *Society of Hospital Medicine 2010 media kit.* Available online at: www.hospitalmedicine.org/AM/Template.cfm?Section=Home&CONTENTID=23077&TEMPLATE=/CM/ContentD isplay.cfm.

[9] National Center for Health Statistics, Division of Health Care Statistics. (n.d.). *2008 NAMCS micro-data file documentation.* Hyattsville, MD: Author. Available online at: ftp://ftp.cdc.gov/pub/Health_Statistics/NCHS/Dataset_Documentation/NAMCS/doc08.pdf; Center for Studying Health System Change. 2008 Health Tracking Physician Survey. Washington, DC: Author. Available online at: www.hschange.com/index.cgi?data=04.

[10] Colwill, J. M., Cultice, J. M. and Kruse, R. L. (2008, May-June). Will generalist physician supply meet demands of an increasing and aging population. *Health Affairs*, *27*(3), w232–w241.

[11] In reviewing the NAMCS, as well as the Health Tracking Physician Survey, a number of issues were considered. These surveys use the AMA Masterfile to develop their sampling frames, but data collection for the surveys occurs between 6 months to a year from when the frame was developed. Thus, for example, some cases out of scope at data collection (e.g., retired, deceased, unlicensed, or having left the United States) that were active on the frame may have become out of scope between frame development and data collection. Similarly, with its focus on office-based practice, some cases in the NAMCS defined as out of scope, such as physicians in institutional settings like school-based clinics, might appropriately be counted in estimates of PCPs. Nonetheless, even with these qualifications, the annual NAMCS—coupled with findings in the single Health Tracking Physician Survey—indicated further downscaling of the physician estimate was appropriate. Depending on the categories out of scope in these surveys, the estimate of primary care physicians in 2010 ranges between 200,000 and 210,000.

The midpoint of this range represents an 8-percent reduction to the preliminary estimate, yielding a final estimate of 205,000 for a baseline in modeling projections.

[12] Association of American Medical Colleges, Center for Workforce Studies. (2009, May). Medical school enrollment plans through 2013: Analysis of the 2008 AAMC survey. Washington, DC: Author.

[13] Brotherton, S. E. and Etzel, S. I. (2010). Graduate medical education, 2009-2010. *Journal of the American Medical Association*, *304*(11), 1255–1270.

[14] Jolly, P., Erikson, C. and Garrison, G. (2013). U.S. graduate medical education and physician specialty choice. *Academic Medicine*, *88*(4), 468-474.

[15] DeRosier, A. and Lischka, T.A. (2012). Osteopathic graduated medical education 2012. *Journal of the American Osteopathic Association*, *112*(4), 196-203.

[16] Brotherton, S. E. and Etzel, S. I. (2010). Graduate medical education, 2009-2010. *Journal of the American Medical Association*, *304*(11), 1255–1270.

[17] Association of American Medical Colleges. Medical School Graduation Questionnaire: 2013 All schools summary report. (2013). Washington, DC: Author. Available online at: www.aamc.org/download/350998/data/2013gqallschoolssummaryreport.pdf.

[18] Johnson, N. J., Sorlie, P. D. and Backlund, E. (1999). The impact of specific occupation on mortality in the U.S. National Longitudinal Mortality Study. *Demography*, *36*(3), 355–367.

[19] Agency for Healthcare Research and Quality. (2011, October). *The number of nurse practitioners and physician assistants practicing primary care in the United States: Primary care workforce facts and stats no. 2* (AHRQ Publication No. 12-P001-3-EF). Rockville, MD: Author. Available online at: www.ahrq.gov/research/pcwork2.pdf.

[20] Fang, D., Tracy, C. and Bednash, G. D. (2012). *2011-2012 enrollment and graduations in baccalaureate and graduate programs in nursing*. Washington, DC: American Association of Colleges of Nursing.

[21] Analysis of the 2008 National Sample Survey of Registered Nurses by HRSA's National Center. See also Health Resources and Services Administration. (2010, September). Advanced practice registered nurses [Chapter 5]. In *The registered nurse population: Findings from the 2008 National Sample Survey of Registered Nurses*. Rockville, MD: Author. Available online at: http://bhpr.hrsa.gov/healthworkforce/rnsurveys/rnsurvey final.pdf; Agency for Healthcare Research and Quality. (2011, October). *The number of nurse practitioners and physician assistants practicing primary care in the United States: Primary care workforce facts and stats no. 2* (AHRQ Publication No. 12-P001-3-EF). Rockville, MD: Author. Available online at: www.ahrq.gov/research/pcwork2.pdf.

[22] In 2006, there were an estimated 4,800 new PA graduates, growing to about 6,000 in 2010, representing a mean annual increase in new graduates of 240. A constant increase of 200 new graduates annually was applied in the projection with the assumption that the rate of growth between 2006 and 2010 may decline slightly after 2010. See Physician Assistant Education Association. (2010, October). *26th annual report on physician assistant educational programs*. Presentation on preliminary data, 2009-2010. Baltimore, MD: Author. Available online at: www.paeaonline.org/index.php?ht=a/GetDocument Action/i/114396; Physician Assistant Education Association. (2008). *23rd annual report on physician assistant educational programs in the United States, 2006-2007* (p. 52). Alexandria, VA: Author. Available online at: www.paeaonline.org/index.php?ht=a/GetDocumentAction/i/3520.)

[23] Program data from the Accreditation Review Commission on Education for the Physician Assistant, Inc. are available online at: www.arc-pa.org/acc_programs/program_data.html.

[24] From a sample of PAs, AAPA estimated the universe of PAs around 83,500 in 2010, of which 31 percent were in primary care with 2 percent with specialty unknown. (American Academy of Physician Assistants. (2011). *Physician assistant census report: Results from the 2010 AAPA census*. Alexandria, VA: Author. Available online at: www.aapa.org/uploadedFiles/2010%20Census%20Report%20National%20_Final.pdf.)

[25] According to findings from the 2007 NAMCS, in 67.6 percent of all visits to physician offices, the patient was to return for another visit at a specified time. The visit disposition in 25.1 percent of the visits was to return if needed, while in 7.4 percent of the visits, the patient was referred to another physician. See Hsiao, C. J., Cherry, D. K., Beatty, P. C. and Rechtsteiner, E. A. (2010). National Ambulatory Medical Care Survey: 2007 summary. *National health statistics reports* (No. 27, Table 27). Hyattsville, MD: National Center for Health Statistics.

[26] For information on HPSA designation, see www.hrsa.gov/shortage.

[27] Freed, G. L. and Stockman, J. A. (2009). Oversimplifying primary care supply and shortages. *Journal of the American Medical Association*, *301*(18), 1920–1922.

[28] Shipman, S. A. (2010, February). Attempting to meet our nation's pediatric workforce needs. *Pediatric Annals*, *39*(2), 89–96.

[29] National Center for Health Statistics (NCHS), Division of Health Care Statistics. National Ambulatory Medical Care Survey. Hyattsville, MD: Author. Available online at: www.cdc.gov/nchs/ahcd.htm. See also National Center for Health Statistics, Division of Health Care Statistics. (n.d.). National Hospital Medical Care Survey. Hyattsville, MD: Author. Available online at: www.cdc.gov/nchs/ahcd.htm and Agency Healthcare Research and Quality, Healthcare Cost and Utilization Project. *Nationwide Inpatient Sample*. Rockville, MD: Author. Available online at: www.hcup-us.ahrq.gov/nisoverview.jsp.

[30] The age categories are 0 to 5, 6 to 17, 18 to 20, 21 to 44, 45 to 64, 65 to 74, and 75 years and older. The race/ethnicity categories are non-Hispanic (NH) White, NH Black, NH other, and Hispanic. The insurance categories are commercially insured under age 65, publically insured (with the age 65 and older population primarily consisting of Medicare patients), and uninsured.

[31] These projections assume that all states will expand Medicaid coverage as authorized by the Affordable Care Act because the projections were developed before the decision of the Supreme Court making the expansion optional. Since the number of states that will expand eligibility for Medicaid is unknown, the projections have not been revised. To the extent that some states do not expand eligibility, the projections will overestimate primary care demand.

[32] Since preparation of these projections, in December of 2012, the U.S. Census Bureau has published new projections of the U.S. population for 2020. The newer projections project a slightly slower rate of overall population growth. Consequently, the projections may slightly overestimate the growth in demand in 2020.

[33] U.S. Census Bureau. American Community Survey. Available online at: www.census.gov/acs/www/.

[34] Douglas W. Elmendorf. CBO's Analysis of the Major Health Care Legislation Enacted in March 2010. Testimony before the Subcommittee on Health, Committee on Energy and Commerce, and U.S. House of Representatives, March 30, 2011. Available online at: www.cbo.gov/publication/22077. The CBO modified its estimate of insurance coverage after the Supreme Court decision on June 28, 2012, that lessened the requirement of states to expand Medicaid in the manner outlined in the Affordable Care Act. The most recent CBO estimate, released in May 2013, has 11 percent ultimately remaining uninsured rather than the 8 percent estimate released at the time that analysis for this report was conducted (see www.cbo.gov/sites/default/files/cbofiles/attachments/44190 EffectsAffordableCareAct HealthInsuranceCoverage 2.pdf). This increase in the percent remaining uninsured might result in less demand, however slight, than projected in this report. See also National Federation of Independent Business v. Sebelius, 132 S. Ct. 2566 (2012).

[35] For more information on obesity and health, including Healthy People 2020 goals for improvement, see www.healthypeople.gov/2020/LHI/nutrition.aspx?tab=overview.

[36] Centers for Disease Control and Prevention. Behavioral Risk Factor Surveillance System Annual Survey Data. Atlanta, GA: Author. Available online at: www.cdc.gov/brfss/annual_data/annual_data.htm.

[37] State was included in the regression analysis since the model used to project future demand calculated estimates at the state level and then aggregated the estimates to produce national totals.

[38] See age-adjusted rates in Flegal, K. M., Carroll, M. D., Ogden, C. L. and Curtin, L. R. (2010). Prevalence and trends in obesity among U.S. adults, 1999-2008. *Journal of the American Medical Association*, *303*(3), 235–241; Centers for Disease Control and Prevention. *Adult obesity facts.* Available online at: www.cdc.gov/obesity/data/adult.html.

[39] Flegal, K. M., Carroll, M. D., Ogden, C. L. and Curtin, L. R. (2010). Prevalence and trends in obesity among U.S. adults, 1999-2008. *Journal of the American Medical Association*, *303*(3), 235–241; Ogden, C. L., Carroll, M. D., McDowell, M. A. and Flegal, K. M. (2007). *Obesity among adults in the United States—No statistically significant change since 2003–2004.* NCHS data brief no 1. Hyattsville, MD: National Center for Health Statistics. Available online at: www.cdc.gov/nchs/data/databriefs/db01.pdf.

[40] See, for example, Hofer, A. N., Abraham, J. N. and Moscovice, I. (2011). Expansion of coverage under the Patient Protection and Affordable Care Act and primary care utilization. *Milbank Quarterly*, *89*(1), 69–89; Huang, E. S. and Finegold, K. (2013). Seven million Americans live in areas where demand for primary care may exceed supply by more than 10 percent. *Health Affairs*, *32*(3), 614–621.

[41] "Negotiated Rulemaking Committee on the Designation of Medically Underserved Populations and Health Professional Shortage Areas: Final Report to the Secretary," October 31, 2011. It is important to note that the Committee did not intend for this weighting to represent the general relative cost or value of NP and PA services compared with physician services. The Committee also acknowledged that these providers often deliver a different set of services than a physician, and that weighting them at 1.0 would overstate the assessment of primary care capacity.

[42] Association of American Medical Colleges, Center for Workforce Studies. (n.d.). 2009 AAMC Physician Survey on Primary Care.

[43] Blanchfield, B. B., Heffernan, J. L., Osgood, B., Sheehan, R. R. and Meyer, G. S. (2011). Saving billions of dollars – and physicians' time – by streamlining billing practices. *Health Affairs*, *29*(6), 1248–1254.

[44] Blumenthal, D. Implementation of the Federal Health Information Technology Initiative. (2011). *New England Journal of Medicine*, *365*(25), 2426–2431.

[45] Physician Assistant Education Association. *17th annual report on physician assistant educational programs in the United States, 2000-2001*. Alexandria, VA: Author. Available online at: www.paeaonline.org/index.php?ht=a/GetDocumentAction/i/61838; Physician Assistant Education Association. (2010, October). *26th annual report on physician assistant educational programs*. Presentation on preliminary data, 2009-2010. Baltimore, MD: Author. Available online at: www.paeaonline.org/index.php?ht=a/GetDocument Action/i/114396.

[46] Dill, M., Pankow, S., Erikson, C. and Shipman, S. (2013). Survey shows consumers open to a greater role for physician assistants and nurse practitioners. *Health Affairs, 32*(6), 1135–1142.

In: U.S. Health Care Workforce
Editor: Sheldon T. Barrett

ISBN: 978-1-63485-730-7

Chapter 2

PROJECTING THE SUPPLY OF NON-PRIMARY CARE SPECIALTY AND SUBSPECIALTY CLINICIANS: 2010-2025*

National Center for Health Workforce Analysis

Anticipated changes in the national supply of physicians, advanced practice nurses[1] (APNs), and physician assistants (PAs) in 35 predefined non-primary care specialty and subspecialty fields are presented in this brief (see Table 1). Using the Clinician Specialty Supply Model (CSSDM) future labor supply changes attributable to the changing demographic composition of the future workforce are projected. All supply projections represent provider Full Time Equivalents (FTEs) active in patient care.

KEY FINDINGS

Increased physician supply across non-primary care fields of practice is projected for 2025, although there is substantial variation across fields.

- The supply of physician FTEs in all non-primary care fields is expected to grow overall by 21 percent between 2010 and 2025.

---

* This is an edited, reformatted and augmented version of a report issued by the U.S. Department of Health and Human Services, Health Resources and Services Administration, July 2014.

- Large growth is projected in some fields (physical medicine and rehabilitation, emergency medicine) while losses are projected in a few others (critical care medicine, occupational medicine, thoracic surgery).
- The *per capita* supply of physicians is projected to vary. Per capita declines are projected in the fields of cardiology, psychiatry and general surgery; whereas per capita growth is projected within the pediatric subspecialties and in obstetrics-gynecology.

The supply of non-primary care APNs is expected to grow more rapidly than physicians.

- Between 2010 and 2025, the supply of non-primary care APN FTEs is expected to grow by 141 percent overall, with growth anticipated in every field where these providers are represented. Changes in the non-primary care APN supply somewhat mirror those of physicians, with the greatest growth expected in the fields of physical medicine and rehabilitation, and emergency medicine.
- The *per capita* supply of APNs is projected to increase across all non-primary care specialties with the greatest increases expected in obstetrics-gynecology and pediatric subspecialties.
- Because of the data sources used, the number of APNs working in 5 of 11 surgical specialties (colorectal surgery, ophthalmology, otolaryngology, plastic surgery, vascular surgery), and in 3 other fields of practice (pathology, preventive medicine, and radiation oncology) are unobtainable.

The supply of non-primary care PAs is also projected to grow more rapidly than physicians, but less than APNs.

- The supply of non-primary care PAs is projected to more than double by 2025, with high rates of growth anticipated in almost all fields of (non-primary care) practice. The anticipated changes in the supply of PAs by field parallels the changes seen with physicians, with particularly high levels of growth projected in the fields of physical medicine and rehabilitation, emergency medicine, and pediatric subspecialties.

- The *per capita* supply of PAs is projected to increase across all fields examined, with obstetrics-gynecology and the pediatric subspecialties expected to have the greatest increases.
- Because of the data sources used the number of PAs specializing in preventive medicine are unobtainable.

BACKGROUND

Physicians, following graduation from medical school and before entering their clinical practice, generally complete *specialty* residency training in either primary care or non-primary care fields. For the latter, much of the training and subsequent focus of clinical practice is within a condition-specific subpopulation of patients. Physicians may then opt, after residency training, to complete additional *subspecialty* fellowship training within a concentrated (non-primary care) clinical area before entering practice. The focus of this report is on the physician workforce who are trained and practice in non-primary care specialties and subspecialties, and advanced practice nurses and physician assistants in these same fields.

RESULTS

Trends in Provider Supply: Of the total of 771,900 U.S. physicians active in patient care in 2010, approximately 498,800 (65 percent of the total) are estimated to be practicing in non-primary care fields.

After accounting for differences in labor supply due to the changing demographic composition of the future providers (including the proportion in part-time roles), it is estimated that the supply of FTE non-primary care physicians in 2025 will increase by 21 percent (from 498,800 to 602,700 FTEs); that of APNs will increase by 141 percent (from 126,900 to 306,000 FTEs); and that of PAs will increase by 108 percent (from 52,500 to 109,300 FTEs).

As a result of the rapid growth in the supply of APNs and PAs, the composition of the non-primary care clinical workforce is expected to change in 2025 (Exhibit 1).

Table 1. Non-primary care specialty and subspecialty fields of practice examined

Non-primary care medical specialties	Medical subspecialties	Surgical specialties	Surgical subspecialties
Anesthesiology	Allergy-Immunology	General Surgery	Colorectal Surgery
Dermatology	Cardiology	Neurological Surgery	Thoracic Surgery
Emergency Medicine	Critical Care Medicine	Ophthalmology	Vascular Surgery
Neurology	Endocrinology	Orthopedic Surgery	Other surgical subspecialties[2]
Obstetrics-Gynecology	Gastroenterology	Otolaryngology	
Occupational Medicine	Hematology-Oncology	Plastic Surgery	
Pathology	Infectious Disease	Urology	
Physical Medicine and Rehabilitation	Nephrology Pediatric Subspecialties		
Preventive Medicine	Pulmonology		
Psychiatry	Rheumatology		
Radiation Oncology			
Radiology			
Other patient care[3]			

Source: The American Board of Medical Specialties at http://www.abms.org/Who We Help/Physicians/specialties.aspx.

Supply of Non-primary Care Specialty and Subspecialty Physicians: By 2025, physician FTE supply within focused (non-primary care) fields of practice is projected to increase by 24 percent in non-primary care medical specialties, 21 percent in medical subspecialties, and 14 percent in surgical fields. Despite these overall trends, the projected growth of physicians within certain specific fields is variable (Table 2). There are large growth increases in neurological surgery and otolaryngology, and declines predicted in thoracic surgery. Among the non-surgical fields, some remain largely stable in their supply (allergy-immunology, cardiology, and psychiatry) while others show high projected growth (the pediatric subspecialties, emergency medicine, and physical medicine and rehabilitation) or large declines (critical care medicine and occupational medicine).

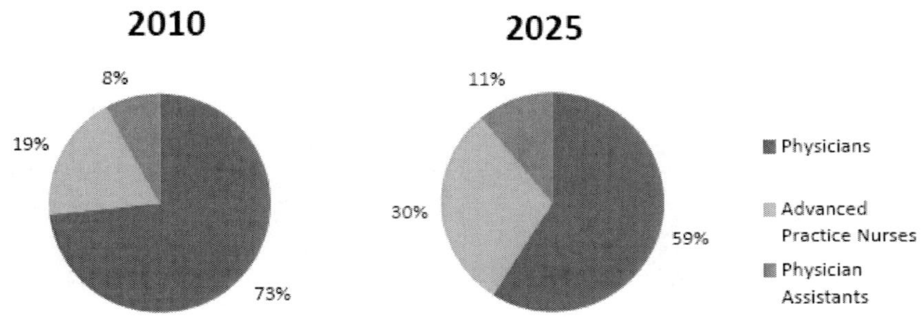

Exhibit 1. Composition of Non-Primary Care Specialty and Subspecialty Clinician Workforce in 2010 and 2025.

Table 2. Projected Changes in the FTE Supply* of Non-Primary Care Specialty and Subspecialty Physicians, 2010-2025

	FTE Supply (2010)	*Projected FTE Supply (2025)*	*Percent Change, 2010 to 2025*	*FTE Supply per 100,000 (2010)*	*Projected FTE Supply per 100,000 (2025)*	*Change, 2010 to 2025#*
Non-primary care medical specialties	*271,700*	*336,800*	*24*	*87.8*	*91.1*	*3.3*
Anesthesiology	46,000	54,800	19	14.9	14.8	0.0
Dermatology	11,500	15,500	35	3.7	4.2	0.5
Emergency Medicine	36,000	55,400	54	11.6	15.0	3.3
Neurology	14,500	20,400	40	4.7	5.5	0.8
Obstetrics-Gynecology	42,400	49,300	16	68.0	72.0	4.0
Occupational Medicine	1,700	1,100	-37	0.6	0.3	-0.3
Pathology	17,800	19,700	11	5.7	5.3	-0.4
Physical Medicine and Rehabilitation	10,400	17,100	64	3.4	4.6	1.3

Table 2. (Continued)

	FTE Supply (2010)	*Projected FTE Supply (2025)*	*Percent Change, 2010 to 2025*	*FTE Supply per 100,000 (2010)*	*Projected FTE Supply per 100,000 (2025)*	*Change, 2010 to 2025#*
Preventive Medicine	2,700	3,100	13	0.9	0.8	0.0
Psychiatry	44,200	46,500	5	14.3	12.6	-1.7
Radiation Oncology	4,700	6,200	32	1.5	1.7	0.2
Radiology	37,100	46,200	25	12.0	12.5	0.5
Other patient care	2,800	1,500	-46	0.9	0.4	-0.5
Medical subspecialties	109,900	132,700	21	35.5	35.9	0.4
Allergy-Immunology	4,000	4,046	2	1.3	1.1	-0.2
Cardiology	25,300	26,623	5	8.2	7.2	-1.0
Critical Care Medicine	1,600	1,410	-11	0.5	0.4	-0.1
Endocrinology	5,400	6,604	23	1.7	1.8	0.1
Gastroenterology	13,000	14,481	11	4.2	3.9	-0.3
Hematology-Oncology	12,500	15,403	23	4.0	4.2	0.1
Infectious Disease	6,400	7,872	23	2.1	2.1	0.1
Nephrology	8,400	10,059	20	2.7	2.7	0.0
Pediatric Subspecialties	17,700	27,500	55	23.9	35.2	11.3
Pulmonology	11,000	13,195	20	3.6	3.6	0.0
Rheumatology	4,600	5,505	19	1.5	1.5	0.0
Surgical specialties	104,000	118,600	14	33.6	32.1	-1.5
General Surgery	28,700	30,400	6	9.3	8.2	-1.0
Neurological Surgery	5,500	7,400	34	1.8	2.0	0.2
Ophthalmology	18,000	19,600	9	5.8	5.3	-0.5
Orthopedic Surgery	24,400	28,700	17	7.9	7.8	-0.1
Otolaryngology	9,800	12,000	23	3.2	3.2	0.1
Plastic Surgery	7,600	9,000	19	2.5	2.4	0.0
Urology	10,100	11,500	14	3.3	3.1	-0.1
Surgical	13,10	14,600	11	4,2	3.9	-0.3

	FTE Supply (2010)	*Projected FTE Supply (2025)*	*Percent Change, 2010 to 2025*	*FTE Supply per 100,000 (2010)*	*Projected FTE Supply per 100,000 (2025)*	*Change, 2010 to 2025#*
subspecialties						
Colorectal Surgery	1,500	1,800	19	0.5	0.5	0.0
Thoracic Surgery	4,400	3,300	-24	1.4	0.9	-0.5
Vascular Surgery	2,900	3,600	26	0.9	1.0	0.0
Other surgical subspecialties	4,400	5,800	34	1.4	1.6	0.2

* FTE supply rounded to the nearest hundred; 1 FTE represents 1 provider who works average number of hours in the base year.

Numbers may not add-up due to rounding.

Although the *per capita* supply of physicians, on average across all non-primary care fields, remains generally stable in proportion to projected population growth (from 161 per 100,000 in 2010 to 163 per 100,000 in 2025), some specific fields experience large increases (the pediatric subspecialties and obstetrics-gynecology) and some fields may see decreases of 1 to 2 FTEs per 100,000 (general surgery, psychiatry, and cardiology). In all surgical fields combined, it is projected that there will be 1.9 fewer physician FTEs per 100,000 in 2025 than in 2010.

Supply of Non-Primary Care Specialty and Subspecialty APNs: Between 2010 and 2025, the APN supply in focused (non-primary care) fields is projected to grow in all areas of practice[4] – by 213 percent in medical subspecialties, 118 percent in non-primary care medical specialties, and 181 percent across all surgical fields (Table 3). Currently, only a small proportion of all APNs specialize in surgical fields (7 percent), and this is anticipated to increase by 1 percent to 8 percent in 2025. The high proportion of APNs in non-primary care medical specialties in 2010 will see a slight decrease by 2025 (from 73 to 66 percent), with a small increase in representation in medical subspecialty fields (from 20 to 26 percent). The high representation of APNs in the non-primary care medical specialties is almost exclusively due to the certified registered nurse anesthetist (CRNA) and certified nurse midwife (CNM) supply, which together constitute over 50 percent of the non-primary care APN workforce. The large gains in FTEs in the projected supply of APNs translate into significant increases in *per capita* numbers of APNs by 2025.

Table 3. Projected Changes in the FTE Supply* of Non-Primary Care Specialty and Subspecialty APNs, 2010-2025

	FTE Supply (2010)	*Projected FTE Supply (2025)*	*Percent Change, 2010 to 2025*	*FTE Supply per 100,000 (2010)*	*Projected FTE Supply per 100,000 (2025)*	*Change, 2010 to 2025#*
Non-primary care medical specialties	*92,700*	*201,800*	*118*	*30.0*	*54.6*	*24.6*
Anesthesiology	43,900	82,000	87	14.2	22.2	8.0
Dermatology	1,300	4,400	241	0.4	1.2	0.8
Emergency Medicine	5,600	21,700	287	1.8	5.9	4.0
Neurology	1,300	4,800	259	0.4	1.3	0.9
Obstetrics-Gynecology	23,200	53,600	131	37.2	78.2	41.0
Occupational Medicine	2,100	3,300	55	0.7	0.9	0.2
Pathology	-	-	-	-	-	-
Physical Medicine and Rehabilitation	700	2,900	317	0.2	0.8	0.6
Preventive Medicine	-	-	-	-	-	-
Psychiatry	7,000	17,900	156	2.3	4.8	2.6
Radiation Oncology	-	-	-	-	-	-
Radiology	600	1,900	213	0.2	0.5	0.3
Other patient care	7,000	9,500	35	2.3	2.6	0.3
Medical subspecialties	*25,400*	*79,500*	*213*	*8.2*	*21.5*	*13.3*
Allergy-Immunology	300	900	154	0.1	0.2	0.1
Cardiology	5,400	14,200	165	1.7	3.8	2.1
Critical Care Medicine	1,200	2,600	119	0.4	0.7	0.3
Endocrinology	1,600	5,000	215	0.5	1.3	0.8
Gastroenterology	1,800	4,900	178	0.6	1.3	0.8
Hematology-Oncology	4,300	13,500	215	1.4	3.7	2.3
Infectious Disease	900	2,800	214	0.3	0.8	0.5
Nephrology	1,000	3,200	210	0.3	0.9	0.5
Pediatric	7,500	27,900	274	10.0	35.6	25.6

	FTE Supply (2010)	Projected FTE Supply (2025)	Percent Change, 2010 to 2025	FTE Supply per 100,000 (2010)	Projected FTE Supply per 100,000 (2025)	Change, 2010 to 2025#
Subspecialties						
Pulmonology	1,200	3,600	205	0.4	1.0	0.6
Rheumatology	400	1,100	202	0.1	0.3	0.2
Surgical specialties	*5,100*	*15,000*	*194*	*1.6*	*4.1*	*2.4*
General Surgery	1,500	4,200	172	0.5	1.1	0.6
Neurological Surgery	1,100	3,700	236	0.4	1.0	0.6
Ophthalmology	-	-	-	-	-	-
Orthopedic Surgery	1,700	5,000	192	0.6	1.4	0.8
Otolaryngology	-	-	-	-	-	-
Plastic Surgery	-	-	-	-	-	-
Urology	700	2,100	184	0.2	0.6	0.3
Surgical subspecialties	*3,700*	*9,700*	*3,700*	*1.2*	*2.6*	*1.4*
Colorectal Surgery	-	-	-	-	-	-
Thoracic Surgery	1,800	3,400	1,800	0.6	0.9	0.3
Vascular Surgery	-	-	-	-	-	-
Other surgical subspecialties	1,900	6,300	234	0.6	1.7	1.1

* FTE supply rounded to the nearest hundred; 1 FTE represents 1 provider who works average number of hours in the base year.

Numbers may not add-up due to rounding.

Supply of Non-Primary Care Specialty and Subspecialty PAs: The PA supply was estimated to be 9,100 in medical subspecialties, 20,400 in surgical specialties, and 23,000 in non-primary care medical specialty areas. By 2025, the PA supply is projected to grow by 110 percent (to 19,000 FTEs) in medical subspecialties, by 99 percent (to 40,500 FTEs) in surgical specialties, and by 117 percent (to 49,900 FTEs) in non-primary care medical specialty areas (Table 4).

Despite some differential growth rates, the distribution of PAs among these broad non-primary care specialty groupings is not expected to change significantly during the projection period. In 2025, PAs in non-primary care specialty areas will constitute 46 percent of the PA non-primary care workforce (previously 44 percent), medical subspecialties will constitute 17 percent (unchanged), and the remaining 37 percent will be in surgical fields (previously 39 percent).

Fields with the highest projected growth for PAs are physical medicine and rehabilitation (193 percent), emergency medicine (172 percent), and the pediatric subspecialties (185 percent). The non-primary care specialty area with the lowest anticipated growth is occupational medicine – with 9 percent growth in FTE supply predicted from 2010 to 2025. Data sources used in these projections identified no PAs working in the field of preventive medicine.

Similar to APNs, the rapid growth of a young PA workforce results in projections where the expected supply of providers exceeds population growth. Therefore, the *per capita* availability of PAs increases in almost all non-primary care fields by 2025.

Table 4. Projected Changes in the FTE Supply[*] of Non-Primary Care Specialty and Subspecialty PAs, 2010-2025

	FTE Supply (2010)	Projected FTE Supply (2025)	Percent Change, 2010 to 2025	FTE Supply per 100,000 (2010)	Projected FTE Supply per 100,000 (2025)	Change, 2010 to 2025[#]
Non-primary care medical specialties	23,000	49,900	117	7.4	13.5	6.1
Anesthesiology	1,100	2,400	110	0.4	0.6	0.3
Dermatology	2,600	6,200	139	0.8	1.7	0.8
Emergency Medicine	9,200	25,000	172	3.0	6.8	3.8
Neurology	500	1,200	153	0.2	0.3	0.2
Obstetrics-Gynecology	2,100	4,300	108	3.3	6.2	2.9
Occupational Medicine	1,800	2,000	9	0.6	0.5	-0.1
Pathology	0	0	104	<0.1	<0.1	<0.1
Physical Medicine and	600	1,800	193	0.2	0.5	0.3
Rehabilitation						
Preventive Medicine	-	-	-	-	-	-
Psychiatry	1,200	2,300	88	0.4	0.6	0.2
Radiation Oncology	200	400	131	0.1	0.1	0.1
Radiology	600	1,400	120	0.2	0.4	0.2

	FTE Supply (2010)	Projected FTE Supply (2025)	Percent Change, 2010 to 2025	FTE Supply per 100,000 (2010)	Projected FTE Supply per 100,000 (2025)	Change, 2010 to 2025#
Other patient care	3,100	2,900	-5	1.0	0.8	-0.2
Medical subspecialties	9,100	19,000	110	2.9	5.2	2.2
Allergy-Immunology	400	800	79	0.1	0.2	0.1
Cardiology	2,800	5,100	86	0.9	1.4	0.5
Critical Care Medicine	400	500	54	0.1	0.1	0.0
Endocrinology	400	800	122	0.1	0.2	0.1
Gastroenterology	1,200	2,300	96	0.4	0.6	0.2
Hematology-Oncology	1,400	3,000	121	0.4	0.8	0.4
Infectious Disease	400	1,000	121	0.1	0.3	0.1
Nephrology	400	900	117	0.1	0.2	0.1
Pediatric Subspecialties	1,200	3,300	185	1.6	4.2	2.7
Pulmonology	400	800	115	0.1	0.2	0.1
Rheumatology	200	500	112	0.1	0.1	0.1
Surgical specialties	15,200	31,400	107	4.9	8.5	3.6
General Surgery	2,400	4,600	91	0.8	1.2	0.5
Neurological Surgery	1,800	4,200	137	0.6	1.1	0.6
Ophthalmology	100	200	91	<0.1	0.1	<0.1
Orthopedic Surgery	8,600	17,700	105	2.8	4.8	2.0
Otolaryngology	600	1,400	116	0.2	0.4	0.2
Plastic Surgery	600	1,300	106	0.2	0.4	0.2
Urology	1,000	2,100	99	0.3	0.6	0.2
Surgical subspecialties	5,200	9,000	75	1.7	2.4	0.8
Colorectal Surgery	100	200	109	<0.1	<0.1	<0.1
Thoracic Surgery	2,900	3,800	31	0.9	1.0	0.1
Vascular Surgery	500	1,100	118	0.2	0.3	0.1
Other surgical subspecialties	1,700	4,000	135	0.6	1.1	0.5

* FTE supply rounded to the nearest hundred; 1 FTE represents 1 provider who works average number of hours in the base year.

Numbers may not add-up due to rounding.

Limitations

This report projects future labor supply changes attributable to the changing demographic composition of the future health workforce. Numerous factors can influence the future supply of health care providers, many of which cannot be easily predicted or modeled. For example, the supply projection methodology cannot predict or incorporate hypothetical new trends in specialty choice by health professions graduates, which can develop in response to changing labor market conditions or other factors. New policies and programs for the training of clinicians, such as emerging models for graduate medical education (GME) financial support that target specialty fields by need or shortage, may influence the specialty distribution of future clinicians. The projections in this brief do not account for health system changes that may improve the efficiency and adequacy of the national provider supply, meaning that potentially fewer providers may be needed to deliver care. These include future system-level changes that cannot be accurately anticipated – such as improvements in technology, practice patterns (such as team-based care models), or service delivery (such as medical homes and accountable care organizations). Finally, these national level projections do not take into account known variations in the distribution of providers at subnational levels, such as in rural and remote areas, or in other regions that are noted to be medically underserved.

Conclusions

This study estimated the *relative supply* of non-primary care clinical workforce in 2025 compared to 2010 under prevalent conditions, accounting only for labor supply changes attributable to the changing demographic composition of the future workforce. The vast majority of non-primary care fields are expected to see some growth, but these projections suggest considerable variations both by profession and by specialty area.

Although the overall supply of non-primary care physicians is expected to increase by 2025, the projected change in physician FTEs is highly variable across areas of specialization. The *per capita* numbers of physicians in non-surgical fields is projected to increase in 2025, but is projected to decline for surgical fields. The supply of physicians in some critical core non-primary care specialty service areas, such as in psychiatry and general surgery, may not keep up with population growth. On the other hand, the rapid growth in the APN and PA workforce is projected to be sufficient to maintain or raise the *per capita* supply of non-primary care specialty providers across all fields in which they are represented.

APPENDIX. ABOUT THE MODEL

The Clinical Specialty Supply Model (CSSDM) is a projection model that uses the stock and flow approach to estimate the future supply of clinicians by specialty (Exhibit 2). The model considers a variety of factors that may impact the supply of clinicians such as the effect of the changing demographic composition of the future workforce.

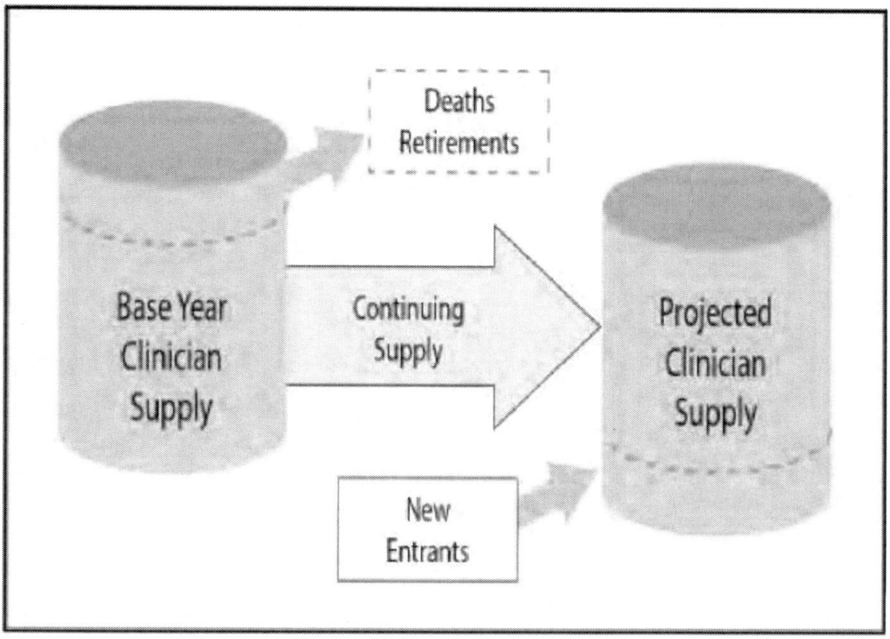

Exhibit 2. Overview of the Clinical Specialty Supply Model.

Clinician supply: Physicians, physician assistants (PAs), nurse practitioners (NPs), certified registered nurse anesthetists (CRNAs), and certified nurse midwives (CNMs) are included in the projection. Data on the number of active clinical providers by age, sex, and specialty are projected forward using age-sex specific attrition rates.[5] Future entrants to the clinical workforce estimated from the expected number of trainees in different profession are based on assumptions regarding the future size and demographic composition of graduating cohorts and include a continuation of the past trends in specialty choices among clinicians. Specifically,

$$C_t = C_0 + En_t - (C_0 * A_0),$$

where C_t represents the projected clinician supply, C_0 represents the current supply of clinicians, En_t represents the number of new trainee entrants, and A_0 represents the attrition rate.

Baseline counts of physicians by age, sex, and specialty are from the 2010 American Medical Association (AMA) physician master file. Physicians who provide direct patient care in the U.S., regardless of the care setting, are included along with residents. Using the equation above, the baseline physician counts are projected forward using age-sex specific attrition rates.[6] Future entrants to the medical profession are estimated from the expected number of graduates from U.S. medical schools and the expected number of total GME training positions. Past trends in specialization from AMA data are used to project the specialty distribution of future cohorts of physicians.

The number of graduate medical education (GME) training slots has been a driver of the total number of new entrants to the physician workforce. In keeping with the recent statistics[7], the projections assume that GME positions will grow by about 1 percent per year up until 2020.

Data from HRSA's 2012 National Survey of Nurse Practitioners (NSSNP) were used to estimate the baseline supply of NPs in patient care by age, sex, and specialty. The 2010 supply of CRNAs active in patient care by age and sex is derived from data provided by the National Board of Certified Registered Nurse Anesthetists. The 2010 American Midwifery Certification Board (AMCB) data were used to estimate the number of available CNMs by age and sex at baseline. Data from these two sources suggest that recent nursing graduate cohorts have been growing by 6[8] and 10 percent.[9] The projections assume a continuation of these rates up until 2017 and no further change in training positions after that. In addition, it is assumed that the American College of Nurse Midwives' strategic goal of 1,000 new graduates by 2015 will be met.

The age-sex distribution of PAs was derived from the 2010 National Commission on Certification of Physician Assistants (NCCPA) and the specialty distribution from the American Association of Physician (AAPA)

Master file. Numbers of new entrants into this profession are projected assuming a continuation of the 5 percent growth in PA graduates observed in the recent past.[10] As with physicians and APNs, the future supply of PAs is projected forward using attrition rates and the expected number of new entrants to the workforce.

The model produces two measures of future clinician supply: counts and relative FTE. Because clinician productivity, in terms of hours worked, depends on the age and sex of a clinician, the changing age-sex distribution of future clinicians have implications for service availability. Data on the average numbers of hours worked by clinicians of different age-sex groups calculated from the 2005-2010 American Community Survey were used to adjust the total number FTEs that would be available in 2025 relative to the current supply.

Per capita FTE supply in 2010 and the projected *per capita* FTE supply in 2025 were calculated from 2010 census data [11] and projected population for 2025 from the U.S. Census Bureau.[12] The *per capita* calculations for obstetrics-gynecology utilized population data from 2010 and 2025 projections of women between 15 and 44 years of age. Those for pediatric subspecialties utilized population data from 2010 and 2025 projections of all persons less than 18 years of age.

End Notes

[1] APNs included in this study are nurse practitioners (NPs), certified registered nurse anesthetists (CRNAs), and certified nurse midwives (CNMs).

[2] This includes Abdominal Surgery, Critical care Surgery, Dermatologic Surgery, Head and Neck Surgery, Hand Surgery, Pediatric Surgery, Surgical Oncology, Traumatic Surgery, and Transplant Surgery.

[3] The term "Other patient care" includes: Addiction Medicine, Epidemiology, Hospice and Palliative Medicine, Legal Medicine, Genetics, Medical Management, Nutrition, Clinical Pharmacology, Phlebology, and Pharmaceutical Medicine.

[4] Data sources used in these projections do not show any APNs working in many of the surgical specialties (colorectal surgery, ophthalmology, otolaryngology, plastic surgery, and vascular surgery) and some non-primary care medical specialties (pathology, preventive medicine, and radiation oncology).

[5] Net attrition rates by age and sex is a combination of age-sex specific mortality rates derived from the U.S. Social Security Administration's published Life tables, Table 6 – Period life tables for Social Security Area by Calendar Year and Sex available at http://www.socialsecurity.gov/OACT/NOTES/as120/LifeTables TBL6 2020.html accessed May 2012, and retirement rates calculated from 2005-2010 American Community Survey.

[6] Net attrition rates by age and sex is a combination of age-sex specific mortality rates derived from the U.S, Social Security Administration's published Life tables, Table 6 – Period life tables for Social Security Area by Calendar Year and Sex available at http://www.socialsecurity.gov/OACT/NOTES/as120/LifeTables TBL6 2020.html accessed May 2012, and retirement rates calculated from 2005-2010 American Community Survey.

[7] Data from Association of American Medical Colleges and American association of Colleges of Osteopathic Medicine 2012.

[8] American Association of Nurse Anesthetists and American Midwifery Certification Board.

[9] American Association of Colleges of Nursing Surveys.

[10] Data from NCCPA report Certified Physician Assistant Population Trends show that the numbers of newly licensed PAs have been increasing by 5percent on average in recent years.

[11] Howden, LM and Meyer, JM "Age and Sex Composition: 2010" 2010 Census Bureau Brief# C2010BR-03, US Census Bureau available at http://www.census.gov/prod/cen2010/briefs/c2010br-03.pdf.

[12] Projections of the Population by Selected Age Groups and Sex for the United States: 2015 to 2060 (NP2012-T2) Source: U.S. Census Bureau, Population Division Release Date: December 2012 downloaded from http://www.census.gov/population/projections/data/national/2012/summarytables.html on May 8, 2014.

In: U.S. Health Care Workforce
Editor: Sheldon T. Barrett

ISBN: 978-1-63485-730-7

Chapter 3

THE FUTURE OF THE NURSING WORKFORCE: NATIONAL- AND STATE-LEVEL PROJECTIONS, 2012-2025*

National Center for Health Workforce Analysis

Using baseline data from 2012 and the Health Resources and Services Administration's (HRSA) Health Workforce Simulation Model, this brief presents national- and state-level projections on the supply of and demand for registered nurses (RNs) and licensed practical/vocational nurses (LPNs) for the entire U.S. in 2025. State-level differences in demographics and the labor market will result in considerable variation in the size and adequacy of the nursing workforce across the country.

KEY FINDINGS

Nationally, the change in RN supply between 2012 and 2025 is projected to outpace demand.

---

* This is an edited, reformatted and augmented version of a report issued by the U.S. Department of Health and Human Services, Health Resources and Services Administration, December 2014.

- Approximately 2.9 million RNs were active in the workforce in 2012. Consistent with standard workforce research methodology, the Health Workforce Simulation Model assumes that the RN demand in 2012 equals the RN supply.
- Assuming RNs continue to train at the current levels and accounting for new entrants and attrition, the RN supply is expected to grow by 952,000 full-time equivalents (FTEs) – from 2,897,000 FTEs in 2012 to 3,849,000 FTEs in 2025 – a 33 percent increase nationally.
- The nationwide demand for RNs, however, is projected to grow by only 612,000 FTEs – from 2,897,000 FTEs in 2012 to 3,509,000 FTEs in 2025 – a 21 percent increase.
- The number of new graduates that entered the workforce has substantially increased from approximately 68,000 individuals in 2001 to more than 150,000 in 2012 and in 2013.
- While not considered in this study, emerging care delivery models, with a focus on managing health status and preventing acute health issues, will likely contribute to new growth in demand for nurses, e.g., nurses taking on new and/or expanded roles in preventive care and care coordination.

Substantial variation at the state level is observed for RN supply and demand.

- Projections at the national level mask a distributional imbalance of RNs at the state level.
- Sixteen states are projected to experience a smaller growth in RN supply relative to their state-specific demand, resulting in a shortage of RNs by 2025; ten of these states are in the West, four are in the South, and two are in the Northeast region.
- States projected to experience the greatest shortfalls in the number of RNs by 2025 are Arizona (with 28,100 fewer RNs than needed) followed by Colorado and North Carolina (each with 12,900 fewer RNs than needed).
- Growth in supply is expected to exceed demand growth in the remaining 34 states, including all of the Midwestern states.

The LPN supply is also projected to outpace demand at the national level.

- Approximately 730,000 LPNs were active in the workforce in 2012. Consistent with standard workforce research methodology, the Health Workforce Simulation Model assumes that the LPN demand in 2012 equals the LPN supply.
- Assuming LPNs continue to train at the current levels and accounting for new entrants and attrition, the LPN supply is expected to grow by 260,900 FTEs – from 730,000 FTEs in 2012 to 990,900 FTEs in 2025 – a 36 percent increase nationally.
- Using current health care utilization patterns, the demand for LPNs is projected to grow by only 28 percent by 2025. The demand for LPNs is projected to grow by 201,000 FTEs – from 730,000 FTEs in 2012 to 931,000 FTEs.
- Similar to the RNs, emerging care delivery models will likely contribute to new growth and demand for LPNs. Since it is too early to determine the impact, this report reflects the demand for the traditional role of the LPNs.

Projected changes in supply and demand for LPNs between 2012 and 2025 vary substantially by state.

- Projections at the national level mask a distributional imbalance of LPNs at the state level.
- Twenty-two states are projected to experience a smaller growth in the supply of LPNs relative to their state-specific demand for LPN services resulting in a shortage of LPNs by 2025. Ten of these states are in the West, five are in the South, five are in the Northeast, and two are in the Midwest.
- Maryland, North Carolina, and Georgia are each expected to fall short by between 7,000 to 8,000 LPNs of their respective 2025 projected demands, whereas Ohio and California each are projected to have an excess of between 20,000 to 25,000 LPNs.

The Evolving Role of the Nursing Workforce.

- The rapidly changing health care delivery system is redefining how care is delivered and the role of the nursing workforce.
- Supply and demand will continue to be affected by numerous factors including population growth and the aging of the nation's population,

overall economic conditions, aging of the nursing workforce, and changes in health care reimbursement.

- Research to model the demand implications of trends in care delivery is ongoing and health workforce projection models will be updated as needed.

BACKGROUND

Nurses make up the single largest health profession in the U.S.[1] They perform a variety of patient care duties and are critical to the delivery of health care services across a wide array of settings, including ambulatory care clinics, hospitals, nursing homes, public health facilities, hospice programs, and home health agencies. Distinctions are made among different types of nurses according to their education, role, and the level of autonomy in practice. Licensed Practical/Vocational Nurses (LPNs) typically receive training for a year beyond high school and, after passing the national NCLEX-PN exam, become licensed to work in patient care. LPNs provide a variety of direct care services including administration of medication, taking medical histories, recording symptoms and vital signs, and other tasks as delegated by registered nurses (RNs), physicians, and other health care providers. RNs usually have a bachelor's degree in nursing, a two year associate's degree in nursing, or a diploma from an approved nursing program. They must also pass a national exam, the NCLEX-RN, before they are licensed to practice. The scope of RN responsibilities is more complex and analytical than that of LPNs. RNs provide a wide array of direct care services, such as administering treatments, care coordination, disease prevention, patient education, and health promotion for individuals, families, and communities. RNs may choose to obtain advanced clinical education and training to become Advanced Practice Nurses (APN). APNs usually have a master's degree, although some complete doctoral-level training, and often focus in a clinical specialty area.

This brief presents national- and state-level projections of the supply of and demand for RNs and LPNs in 2025. Advance practice nurses are not addressed in this nursing-focused report.

RESULTS

Nursing Graduation Rates: The number of new graduates who entered the workforce has substantially increased from approximately 68,000 individuals in 2001 to more than 150,000 in 2012 and in 2013. In 2004, HRSA released projections of RN supply and demand that suggested virtually no growth in supply between 2000 and 2020, with the number of new nurse graduates offsetting the expected number of nurses retiring. [2] At the time, the nation was educating approximately 68,000 nurses annually. The report stated that the U.S. was on a path where demand for RNs would exceed supply in 2020. The recommendation was to increase the number of new graduates to approximately 130,000 annually. Over the next several years, educational capacity was expanded and enrollments were increased in nursing programs (Exhibit 1).

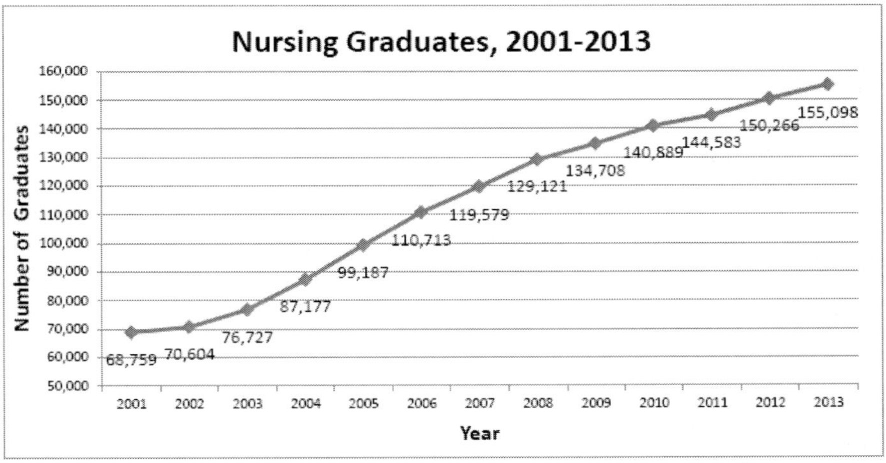

Notes: [a] Data Source: HRSA compilation of data from the National Council of State Boards of Nursing, Exam Statistics and Publications, 2001 to 2013. https://www.ncsbn.org/1232.htm.

Exhibit 1. Number of Nursing Graduates 2001-2013.[a]

National Trends in RN Supply and Demand: Approximately 2.9 million RNs were active in the U.S. workforce in 2012. Trending forward to 2025, close to 2 million new RNs will enter the workforce (assuming new RNs are produced at the current rate) and an estimated 1 million RNs will leave the workforce. This net growth of 952,000 new nurses will result in a national workforce of 3,849,000 RNs by 2025. (Exhibit 2)

Based on 2012 health care delivery and staffing patterns and assuming the current RN demand equals the current RN supply of approximately 2.9 million, the demand for RNs is projected to reach 3.5 million in 2025, an increase of 612,000 RNs. A growth in disease burden attributable to changing patient demographics contributes to an increased demand of 584,000 RNs, and expanded insurance coverage under the Affordable Care Act accounts for a demand of an additional 28,000 RNs.

The greater growth rate of supply (33 percent) over that of demand (21 percent) will result in an excess of 340,000 RNs by 2025.

Exhibit 2. Projected National Supply of and Demand for Registered Nurses

	Registered Nurses
Supply	
Estimated supply, 2012	2,897,000
Estimated supply growth, 2012-2025	952,000
New entrants	1,950,000
Attrition[a]	(998,800)
Change in average work hoursb	800
Projected supply, 2025	3,849,000
Demand[c]	
Estimated demand, 2012	2,897,000
Estimated demand growth, 2012-2025	612,000
Changing demographics	584,000
ACA-related increase in the number of insured	28,000
Projected demand, 2025	3,509,000
Supply in Excess of Demand, 2025	*340,000*

Notes:

[a] Includes RNs who exit to become APNs;

[b] This represents the change in nurse full time equivalents resulting from a change in the demographic composition of the future workforce and the associated effect on average number of hours worked;

[c] The model assumes that demand and supply are equal in 2012.

State Trends in RN Supply and Demand: There is substantial state variation in the projected supply and demand for the RN workforce in 2025.

Exhibit 3. Baseline and Projected Supply of and Demand for Registered Nurse Workforce 2012-2025

	2012	*2025 Projected*		
Region/State	*Supply and Demand*[a]	*Demand*	*Supply*	*Difference*[b]
Northeast				
Connecticut	37,100	41,500	45,200	+3,700
Maine	16,200	17,500	15,800	-1,700
Massachusetts	78,800	85,500	85,900	+400
New Hampshire	15,700	18,000	18,500	+500
New Jersey	84,600	98,500	119,400	+20,900
New York	191,200	212,400	235,800	+23,400
Pennsylvania	145,000	152,600	178,400	+25,800
Rhode Island	12,900	14,000	11,900	-2,100
Vermont	7,400	8,100	8,800	+700
Northeast subtotal	*588,900*	*648,100*	*719,700*	*+71,600*
Midwest				
Illinois	126,900	140,100	149,800	+9,700
Indiana	66,400	71,400	91,600	+20,200
Iowa	34,600	35,300	56,600	+21,300
Kansas	30,300	32,800	47,600	+14,800
Michigan	96,300	104,600	116,000	+11,400
Minnesota	59,300	66,500	84,900	+18,400
Missouri	61,600	67,700	85,000	+17,300
Nebraska	20,900	21,900	22,100	+200
North Dakota	7,400	7,600	10,400	+2,800
Ohio	130,600	137,400	212,800	+75,400
South Dakota	10,000	10,600	14,500	+3,900
Wisconsin	63,300	68,800	78,100	+9,300
Midwest subtotal	*707,600*	*764,700*	*969,400*	*+204,700*
South				
Alabama	50,200	55,700	70,100	+14,400
Arkansas	27,600	31,800	47,700	+15,900
Delaware	10,600	12,500	16,200	+3,700
Florida	171,600	225,500	229,700	+4,200
Georgia	77,300	101,400	94,700	-6,700
Kentucky	47,300	51,000	67,500	+16,500

Exhibit 3. (Continued)

	2012	*2025 Projected*		
Region/State	*Supply and Demand*[a]	*Demand*	*Supply*	*Difference*[b]
Louisiana	41,300	46,500	64,700	+18,200
Maryland	60,600	72,000	59,900	-12,100
Mississippi	32,200	35,800	47,000	+11,200
North Carolina	95,800	120,000	107,100	-12,900
Oklahoma	32,200	37,300	55,000	+17,700
South Carolina	44,600	54,600	54,000	-600
Tennessee	65,000	76,100	92,200	+16,100
Texas	192,000	278,300	284,400	+6,100
Virginia	69,900	87,300	106,700	+19,400
West Virginia	20,600	21,100	29,000	+7,900
South subtotal	*1,038,800*	*1,306,900*	*1,425,900*	*+119,000*
West				
Alaska	5,600	7,300	4,600	-2,700
Arizona	53,000	87,200	59,100	-28,100
California	277,000	393,600	389,900	-3,700
Colorado	42,900	59,000	46,100	-12,900
Hawaii	10,700	13,400	13,200	-200
Idaho	11,700	15,400	16,100	+700
Montana	10,700	12,100	11,300	-800
Nevada	19,400	32,400	24,600	-7,800
New Mexico	15,900	22,100	18,700	-3,400
Oregon	31,300	40,100	34,100	-6,000
Utah	19,700	25,400	31,200	+5,800
Washington	57,800	75,100	68,100	-7,000
Wyoming	4,300	4,900	6,800	+1,900
West subtotal	*560,000*	*788,000*	*723,800*	*-64,200*
US[c]	*2,897,000*	*3,509,000*	*3,849,000*	*+340,000*

Notes:

[a] Projections assume demand and supply are equal in 2012 and nurses remain in their state of training.

[b] Difference = 2025 projected supply – demand. c Includes Washington, D.C.; data for D.C. are not presented separately because the small sample size in American Community Survey (ACS) generated unstable supply estimates.

Despite projections of an excess of RNs at the national level, 16 states are expected to see their supply of RNs outpaced by increases in demand, resulting in shortages. Ten of these states are in the West, four are in the South, and two are in the Northeast U.S. Census Bureau Regions. Midwestern states, on the other hand, are expected to improve the adequacy of their RN supply in 2025. (Exhibit 3)

Arizona is projected to have the largest state-level shortfall of over 28,100 RNs in 2025, followed by Colorado and North Carolina each with 12,900 fewer RNs than will be needed. Maryland and Nevada are also expected to see large declines in the adequacy of their RN workforce. On the other hand, states that currently have some of the largest numbers of RNs (New York, Pennsylvania, Ohio, and Illinois) are projected to experience further improvements in the adequacy of their RN supply relative to 2012.

National Trends in LPN Supply and Demand: Approximately 730,000 LPNs were active in the U.S. workforce in 2012. Trending forward to 2025 using current supply determinants (such as rates of entry, or attrition from the profession) there will be 832,000 new LPNs in the workforce and 571,000 LPNs will leave the workforce. This net growth of 260,900 new nurses will result in a national workforce of 990,900 LPNs by 2025. (Exhibit 4)

Assuming the current LPN demand equals the current LPN supply of 730,000, the demand for LPNs is projected to reach 931,000 by 2025, an increase of 201,000. This growth in demand is driven primarily by an aging population, resulting in increased health service needs. The impact of expanded insurance coverage under the Affordable Care Act is relatively small.

State Trends in LPN Supply and Demand: Assuming LPNs remain in the state where they receive their training, 22 states are projected to see that their LPN supply will be outpaced by demand by 2025 – including 10 states in the West, 5 each in the South and Northeast, and 2 in the Midwest. Arizona, with a projected deficit of 9,590 LPNs, will have the largest shortage. Other states with relatively large projected shortfalls are all in the South: Maryland with an expected shortfall of 7,880 LPNs; North Carolina with a shortfall of 7,760 LPNs; and Georgia with 7,100 fewer LPNs than needed. States currently with a larger LPN workforce (New York, Ohio, Florida, Texas and California) trend towards higher LPN supply relative to demand, with Ohio exhibiting the greatest projected excess supply of 25,240 LPNs by 2025. (Exhibit 5)

Exhibit 4. Projected National Supply and Demand of Licensed Practical Nurses

	Licensed Practical Nurses
Supply	
Estimated supply, 2012	730,000
Estimated supply growth, 2012-2025	260,900
New entrants	832,000
Attrition[a]	(571,000)
Change in average work hours[b]	100
Projected supply, 2025	990,900
Demand[c]	
Estimated demand, 2012	730,000
Estimated demand growth, 2012-2025	201,000
Changing demographics	195,000
ACA-related increases in the number of insured	6,000
Projected demand, 2025	931,000
Supply in Excess of Demand, 2025	*59,000*

Notes:

[a] Includes LPNs who exit to become RNs;

[b] This represents the change in nurse full time equivalents resulting from a change in the demographic composition of the future workforce and the associated effect on average number of hours worked;

[c] The model assumes that demand and supply are equal in 2012.

Exhibit 5. Baseline and Projected Supply of and Demand for the Licensed Practical Nurse Workforce 2012-2025

	2012	*2025 Projected*		
State/Region	*Supply and Demand*[a]	*Demand*	*Supply*	*Difference*[b]
Northeast				
Connecticut	8,300	9,810	11,540	+1,730
Maine	2,150	2,840	1,750	-1,090
Massachusetts	14,020	16,690	14,380	-2,310
New Hampshire	3,930	4,820	4,390	-430
New Jersey	18,500	23,260	36,220	+12,960
New York	45,380	53,470	55,050	+1,580
Pennsylvania	41,380	44,990	42,680	-2,310
Rhode Island	1,640	2,050	930	-1,120
Vermont	1,410	1,800	2,340	+540
Northeast subtotal	*136,710*	*159,730*	*169,280*	*+9,550*

	2012	*2025 Projected*		
State/Region	*Supply and Demand*[a]	*Demand*	*Supply*	*Difference*[b]
Midwest				
Illinois	22,390	27,220	29,360	+2,140
Indiana	18,130	20,230	22,200	+1,970
Iowa	7,980	8,560	16,880	+8,320
Kansas	7,360	8,380	13,460	+5,080
Michigan	20,460	24,100	23,270	-830
Minnesota	15,880	18,630	24,030	+5,400
Missouri	19,430	21,850	23,560	+1,710
Nebraska	5,600	5,800	3,120	-2,680
North Dakota	2,660	2,800	2,950	+150
Ohio	39,340	41,650	66,890	+25,240
South Dakota	1,840	2,090	2,750	+660
Wisconsin	12,120	14,490	15,650	+1,160
Midwest subtotal	*173,190*	*195,800*	*244,120*	*+48,320*
South				
Alabama	13,930	16,110	15,410	-700
Arkansas	12,750	14,250	17,410	+3,160
Delaware	1,940	2,600	4,380	+1,780
Florida	47,270	63,910	65,430	+1,520
Georgia	25,910	33,260	26,160	-7,100
Kentucky	12,110	13,720	17,350	+3,630
Louisiana	15,890	17,900	20,400	+2,500
Maryland	13,150	16,960	9,080	-7,880
Mississippi	11,210	12,550	13,260	+710
North Carolina	20,650	28,180	20,420	-7,760
Oklahoma	15,440	17,180	19,720	+2,540
South Carolina	11,990	15,540	11,630	-3,910
Tennessee	23,330	27,200	27,580	+380
Texas	60,730	85,090	86,230	+1,140
Virginia	23,630	29,630	34,470	+4,840
West Virginia	7,350	7,830	8,380	+550
South subtotal	*317,280*	*401,910*	*397,310*	*-4,600*
West				
Alaska	910	1,480	590	-890
Arizona	8,940	19,090	9,500	-9,590
California	56,100	91,540	112,140	+20,600
Colorado	6,190	11,360	7,230	-4,130
Hawaii	1,590	2,610	2,310	-300
Idaho	3,090	4,320	4,270	-50
Montana	1,800	2,420	2,060	-360
Nevada	3,260	6,950	5,750	-1,200

Exhibit 5. (Continued)

	2012	*2025 Projected*		
State/Region	*Supply and Demand*[a]	*Demand*	*Supply*	*Difference*[b]
New Mexico	3,060	5,210	3,160	-2,050
Oregon	3,500	6,490	6,100	-390
Utah	2,660	4,400	6,510	+2,110
Washington	9,800	15,490	14,290	-1,200
Wyoming	940	1,250	1,540	+290
West subtotal	*101,840*	*172,610*	*175,450*	*2,840*
USc	*730,000*	*931,000*	*990,900*	*59,900*

Notes:

[a] Projections assume demand and supply are equal in 2012 and nurses remain in their state of training.

[b] Difference = 2025 projected supply – demand.

[c] Includes Washington, D.C.; data for D.C. are not presented separately because the small sample size in ACS generated unstable supply estimates.

ALTERNATIVE SCENARIOS

Several alternative scenarios that utilize different assumptions were examined in the preparation of this report. For example, if the demand for RNs returns to pre-recession levels (prior to 2007), then excess capacity is projected to decline from 340,000 to approximately 236,000 RNs by 2025. Adjusting the number of new graduates to approximately 126,000 to 133,000 per year should align supply with the projected demand for services if care delivery patterns were to remain unchanged.

However, since the 1980s, the annual number of nurse graduates has been cyclical and characterized by high growth followed by declines of up to 25%. In an alternative supply and demand scenario if nurses begin retiring two years earlier than pre-recession levels and there is a 10% drop in new graduates, future supply would fall below projected demand resulting in a shortfall of 86,000 RNs in 2025.

Alternatively, if the number of new LPNs educated each year were to decline by 10% relative to current numbers, then projected supply and demand would be in equilibrium in 2025. In another alternative supply and demand scenario if LPNs begin retiring two years earlier than pre-recession levels and there is a 10% drop in new graduates, future supply would fall below projected demand resulting in a shortfall of 19,000 LPNs in 2025.

Therefore, while the evidence in this report points towards the U.S. currently educating slightly more nurses than required to meet future demand, a reduction in people choosing nursing as a career or a combination of factors such as early retirement or increased demand, could be sufficient to erase projected surpluses for RNs and LPNs.

LIMITATIONS

HRSA's Health Workforce Simulation Model operates under several assumptions regarding the current status and future trends in health care utilization and workforce supply. The HRSA Model, like most other health workforce projection models, assumes that the labor market for nurses is currently in balance (i.e., supply and demand in the base year are equal).[3,4] Therefore, the results in this brief reflect changes in the nursing workforce over time relative to a balanced 2012 baseline. The HRSA Model also assumes that the future production of nurses will remain consistent with the current rate. However, there have historically been large swings in enrollment and the resulting labor supply, which, if repeated in the future, would affect the results reported here.

State-level projections require assumptions about the geographic mobility of nurses. Results presented here assume that nurses will practice in states where they have been trained. As a result, many states are projected to have nursing shortages in 2025 despite the fact that, on a national level, there is projected to be an excess of both RNs and LPNs. If, on the other hand, migration were optimal (i.e., nurses were able and willing to migrate to states where the in-state supply did not meet demand), then every state would show a relative surplus of RNs and LPNs in 2025. This accentuates the fact that nursing shortages currently (and in 2025) represent a problem with workforce distribution rather than magnitude. Although there is evidence that some very specialized settings may be facing nurse shortages,[5] this report looks at the nursing profession as a whole and does not look at individual nursing specialty areas (e.g., public health, home health care, etc.) or sites of practice (e.g., nursing homes, ambulatory settings, etc.).

This brief's projections do account for increased utilization of health care services due to expanded insurance coverage under the Affordable Care Act. However, because of the uncertainties in its effects on staffing patterns and the evolving roles of different health professionals on care teams, changes in health care service delivery are not incorporated into the model. If the growing emphasis on care coordination, preventive services, and chronic disease management in care delivery models leads to a greater need for nurses, this brief may underestimate the projected nurse demand.

CONCLUSION

Using the most recently available data on nurse education, labor supply, and retirement patterns, HRSA's Health Workforce Simulation Model projects that by 2025 the supply of RNs and LPNs will grow more than the demand at the national level and for most states. Since 2000, the U.S. has more than doubled the number of RNs educated annually. The current high level of nurse training will add about 2 million new RNs and 800,000 new LPNs into the workforce by 2025, resulting in a national excess of 340,000 RNs and 59,900 LPNs, as compared to 2012. However, distributional patterns for the profession indicate that shortages exist and may persist or worsen in a number of states.

While these projections are consistent with findings in recent studies on RN supply,[6,7] historical experience demonstrates how sensitive enrollment in training programs and the resulting labor supply of nurses are to the job market and economic conditions.[8, 9] For example, the growth of new entrants into the RN workforce is susceptible to the fragile supply of nurse educators.[10]

The HRSA Model estimated a growth in the demand for RNs by 21 percent and LPNs by 28 percent between 2012 and 2025. This growth is comparable to the U.S. Bureau of Labor Statistic's job growth estimate of 19 percent for RNs and 25 percent for LPNs between 2012 and 2022.[11] The state-level estimates derived from the Model are in agreement with recent data[12,13] on RNs which have identified the South and West regions of the country as most vulnerable to RN shortages. Some of the projected declines in nurse supply in these states could be compensated for if nurses from states with an excess of RNs migrate to states with a deficit. However, given the nature of the nurse labor market and state regulatory environment, relaying on migration of nurses may not be adequate. An effort to increase the capacity for states facing potential shortfalls to expand educational opportunities might be one effective strategy to mitigate the geographic variation in nurse supply.

About the Model

The results reported in this brief come from HRSA's new Health Workforce Simulation Model, which is an integrated health professions projection model that estimates the current and future supply of and demand for health care providers.

The supply component of the Model simulates workforce decisions for each provider based on his or her demographics and profession, along with the characteristics of the local or national economy and the labor market. The starting supply, plus new additions to the workforce, minus attrition provides an end of year supply projection, which becomes the starting supply for the subsequent year. This cycle is repeated through 2025. The basic file that underlies the supply analysis contains individual records of the RNs and LPNs in the workforce from the American Community Survey (ACS).

Demand projections for health care services in different care settings are produced by applying regression equations for individuals' health care use on the projected population. The current nurse staffing patterns by care setting are then applied to forecast the future demand for nurses. The population database used to estimate demand consists of records of individual characteristics of a representative sample of the entire U.S. population derived from the ACS, National Nursing Home Survey, and the Behavioral Risk Factor Surveillance System. Using the Census Bureau's projected population and the Urban Institute's state-level estimates of the impact of the Affordable Care Act on insurance coverage,[1, 2] the Model simulates future populations with expected demographic, socioeconomic, health status, health risk and insurance status.

This Model makes projections at the state level, which are then aggregated to the national level. A detailed description of the Model can be found in the accompanying technical documentation available at http://bhw.hrsa.gov/healthworkforce/index.html.

[1] Holahan, J. and Blumberg, L. (2010 January). How would states be affected by health reform? Timely analysis of immediate health policy issues. Retrieved August 2013 from http://www.urban.org/UploadedPDF/412015_affected_by_health_reform.pdf.

[2] Holahan, J. (2014 March) The launch of the Affordable Care Act in selected states: coverage expansion and uninsurance Retrieved August 2013 from http://www.urban.org/uploadedPDF/413036-the-launch-of-the-Affordable-Care-Act-in-selectedstates-coverage-expansion-and-uninsurance.pdf. Washington D.C., The Urban Institute.

Looking to the future, many factors will continue to affect the demand and supply of the nurse workforce including population growth and the aging of the nation's population, overall economic conditions, aging of the nursing workforce, new care delivery models and demand for health services broadly and within specific health care settings, and changes in health care reimbursement.[14] The Affordable Care Act (ACA) is designed to expand the number of people with health insurance coverage and to encourage new value-based models of care. With an emphasis on maintaining health status and preventing acute health crises, these models are providing new opportunities and roles for nurses within the health care delivery system.[15] It is too early to tell whether emerging care delivery models will contribute to a new growth in demand for nurses—e.g., with nurses taking on new and increased roles in prevention and care coordination. Additionally, emerging care delivery models such as Accountable Care Organizations could change the way the LPNs are employed, but there is currently insufficient information to project the extent to which these new delivery models will materially affect the demand for LPNs. Research to model the demand implications of trends in care delivery is ongoing.

The supply and demand projections presented assume that care use and delivery patterns will remain unchanged. However, the health care system continues to evolve in response to changing technology, shifting financial incentives and economic pressures, and efforts to improve care access and quality. The net effects of these and other factors on supply and demand projections will continue to be researched. HRSA will update supply and demand projections as changes emerge in staff utilization patterns, reimbursement policies, health care coverage, scope of practice, health care delivery models, and other labor and economic factors.

End Notes

[1] U.S. Department of Labor, Bureau of Labor Statistics. (2012). Occupational Outlook Handbook, 2012-13 Edition. Washington, D.C.: GPO, U.S. Bureau of Labor Statistics. Retrieved from http://www.bls.gov/ooh/healthcare/registered-nurses.htm; http://www.bls.gov/ooh/healthcare/licensed-practical-and-licensed-vocational-nurses.htm.

[2] U.S. Department of Health and Human Services, Health Resources and Services Administration. (2004). What Is Behind HRSA's Projected Supply, Demand, and Shortage of Registered Nurses? Washington, D.C.: USDHHS, HRSA.

[3] Ono, T., Lafortune, G., Schoenstein, M. (2013). Health workforce planning in OECD countries: a review of 26 projection models from 18 countries. OECD Health Working Papers, No. 62. France: OECD Publishing; 2013:8-11.

[4] Yang, W., Williams, J.H., Hogan, P.F., Bruinooge, S.S., Rodriguez, G.I., Kosty, M.P, Bajorin, D.F., Hanley, A., Muchow, A., McMillan, N., Goldstein, M. (2014). Projected supply of and demand for oncologists and radiation oncologists through 2025: an aging, better-insured population will result in shortage. J Oncol Pract., 10(1):39-45.

[5] American Association of Colleges of Nursing. (2014, April 24). Nursing shortage fact sheet. Retrieved August 21, 2014, from http://www.aacn.nche.edu/media-relations/fact-sheets/nursing-shortage.

[6] Auerbach, D. I., Buerhaus, P. I. and Staiger, D. O. (2014). Registered nurses are delaying retirement, a shift that has contributed to recent growth in the nurse workforce. Health Affairs, 33(8):1474-1480.

[7] Auerbach, D. I., Buerhaus, P. I. and Staiger, D. O. (2011) Registered nurse supply grows faster than projected amid surge in new entrants ages 23-26 Health Affairs, 30(12):2286-2292.

[8] Buerhaus, P.I., Auerbach, D.I. and Staiger, D.O. (2009). The recent surge in nurse employment: causes and implications. Health Affairs, 28(4): w657-w668.

[9] Staiger, D. O., Auerbach, D. I. and Buerhaus, P. I. (2012). Registered nurse labor supply and the recession —are we in a bubble? NEJM, 366(16):1463-1465.

[10] American Association of Colleges of Nursing (2014). Nursing faculty shortage fact sheet. Retrieved September 30, 2014 from http://www.aacn.nche.edu/media-relations/fact-sheets/nursing-faculty-shortage.

[11] U.S. Department of Labor, Bureau of Labor Statistics. (2013, December 19). Occupations with the largest projected number of job openings due to growth and replacement needs, 2012 and projected 2022. Economic News Release Table 8. Retrieved August 19, 2014 from http://www.bls.gov./news.release/ecopro.t08.htm.

[12] Juraschek, S.P., Zhang, X., Ranganathan, V. and Lin, V.W. (2012). United States Registered Nurse Workforce Report Card and Shortage Forecast. American Journal of Medical Quality, 27(3): 241-249.

[13] Buerhaus, P.I., Auerbach, D.I., Staiger, D. O. and Muench, U. (2013). Projections of the long-term growth of the registered nurse workforce: a regional analysis. Nursing Economics, 31(1):13-17.

[14] Institute of Medicine. (2008). Retooling for an aging America, building the health care workforce. Washington (DC): National Academies Press.

[15] Rother, J. and Lavizzo-Mourey, R. (2009). Addressing the nursing workforce: A critical element for health reform. Health Affairs, 28(4), w620-w624.

In: U.S. Health Care Workforce
Editor: Sheldon T. Barrett
ISBN: 978-1-63485-730-7

Chapter 4

HEALTH WORKFORCE PROJECTIONS: HEALTHCARE SUPPORT OCCUPATIONS*

National Center for Health Workforce Analysis

KEY FINDING

Between 2012 and 2025:

- All five healthcare occupations presented in this fact sheet will experience an increase in demand.
- Demand will grow by 20 percent for respiratory therapy technicians, 17 percent for pharmacy technicians, 17 percent for pharmacy aides, 23 percent for occupational therapy assistants and 24 percent for physical therapy assistants.

This fact sheet presents the national demand for select healthcare support occupations for 2012 through 2025 using HRSA's Health Workforce Simulation Model (HWSM).[1] Supply projections are not included due to lack of sufficient data to provide reliable estimates of future supply. Occupations discussed in this fact sheet include respiratory therapy technicians, pharmacy technicians, pharmacy aides, occupational therapy assistants and physical

* This is an edited, reformatted and augmented version of a fact sheet issued by the U.S. Department of Health and Human Services, Health Resources and Services Administration, April 2015.

therapy assistants. While the nuances of modeling demand differ for individual health professions, the basic framework within the HWSM remains the same. The HWSM assumes that demand equals supply in the base year. For demand modeling, the major components include population demographics, health care use patterns (including the influence of the Affordable Care Act health care coverage), and demand for health care providers (translated into Full-Time Equivalents). Over the period studied, the model assumes that current national patterns of service demand remain unchanged within each demographic group.[2] These projections do not account for the geographical distribution of providers which may impact access to care in certain communities.

BACKGROUND

Five healthcare support occupations are discussed in this brief: respiratory therapy technicians, pharmacy technicians, pharmacy aides, occupational therapy assistants, and physical therapy assistants. Respiratory therapy technicians assist respiratory therapists and physicians and provide medical treatment to patients with breathing and cardiopulmonary problems such as asthma or emphysema. Under the direction of other health professionals, they can also provide medical aid to adults that have lungs problems or babies with undeveloped lungs. Respiratory therapy technicians require an associate's degree and need to be registered.

Pharmacy technicians help licensed pharmacists dispense prescription medication. They generally have a high school diploma and learn through on the job training. Pharmacy technicians are regulated in many states. Pharmacy aides perform administrative and customer services tasks in a pharmacy such as recording drug inventory and filing prescriptions, and have no formal education requirements.

Occupational therapy assistants have direct involvement in providing therapy to patients and work under the direction of occupational therapists. Occupational therapy assistants must have an associate's degree and may be certified. In most states, occupational therapy assistants must be licensed. Physical therapist assistants work under the direction and supervision of physical therapists, implementing components of patient care plans, helping obtain outcomes data from physical therapy interventions, and modifying therapies to progress the patient or to ensure patient comfort and safety. Physical therapist assistants must have an associate degree, and many states require licensure.

FINDINGS

There were approximately 13,500 respiratory therapy technicians, 334,400 pharmacy technicians, 42,600 pharmacy aides, 29,500 occupational therapy assistants and 76,500 physical therapy assistants nationally in 2012. Demand for both pharmacy technicians and aides is projected to grow 17 percent between 2012 and 2025 (Exhibit 1). During this same time period, demand for respiratory therapy technicians is projected to increase by 20 percent and occupational therapy assistants by 23 percent. Physical therapy assistants are expected to see the most growth in demand at 24 percent.

Exhibit 1. Estimated Demand for Selected Health Support Occupations in the U.S., 2012 – 2025

	Respiratory therapy technicians	Pharmacy technicians	Pharmacy aides	Occupational therapy assistants	Physical therapy assistants
Demand					
Estimated demand, 2012	13,500	334,400	42,600	29,500	76,500
Total demand growth, 2012-2025:	2,700 (20%)	54,600 (17%)	7,200 (17%)	6,900 (23%)	18,400 (24%)
Changing demographics impact	2,500	45,900	6,000	6,600	17,300
ACA insurance coverage impact	200	8,700	1,200	300	1,100
Projected demand, 2025	16,200	389,000	49,800	36,400	94,900

Factors that influence demand are integrated into the HWSM, including the aging and growth of the U.S. population and the implementation of the Affordable Care Act. The growing elderly population will lead to increased incidence of illness and chronic conditions and greater demand for health care as well as pharmacy services. The Affordable Care Act's emphasis on wellness and prevention will lead to increased use of health resources (impacting all health care occupations overall), and the increase in the number of Americans with prescription drug coverage will lead to increased use in pharmacy services (impacting primarily the pharmacy occupations). Together, these two factors suggest that demand for pharmacy, respiratory, occupational, and physical therapy services will remain high.

About the National Center for Health Workforce Analysis

The National Center for Health Workforce Analysis informs public and private-sector decision-making related to the health workforce by expanding and improving health workforce data, disseminating workforce data to the public, and improving and updating projections of the supply and demand for health workers. For more information about the National Center for Health Workforce Analysis please visit our website at bhw.hrsa.gov/healthworkforce/.

End Notes

[1] This model uses a micro-simulation approach where supply is projected based on the simulation of career choices of individual health workers. Demand for health care services is simulated for a representative sample of the current and future U.S. population based on each person's demographic and socioeconomic characteristics, health-related behavior, and health risk factors that affect their health care utilization patterns. For more information on data and methods, please see BHW HRSA Health Workforce Supply and Demand Simulation Model.

[2] Ono T, Lafortune G, Schoenstein M. "Health workforce planning in OECD countries: a review of 26 projection models from 18 countries." OECD Health Working Papers, No. 62. France: OECD Publishing; 2013:8-11.

In: U.S. Health Care Workforce
Editor: Sheldon T. Barrett

ISBN: 978-1-63485-730-7

Chapter 5

HEALTH WORKFORCE PROJECTIONS: HEALTH TECHNOLOGIST AND TECHNICIAN OCCUPATIONS*

National Center for Health Workforce Analysis

KEY FINDING

Between 2012 and 2025:

- All five health technologist and technician occupations presented in this fact sheet will experience an increase in demand.
- Demand will grow by 24 percent for nuclear medicine technologists, 24 percent for radiologic technologists, 21 percent for diagnostic medical sonographers, 22 percent for medical and clinical laboratory technologists, and 22 percent for medical and clinical laboratory technicians.

This fact sheet presents the national demand for select health technologist and technician occupations for 2012 through 2025 using HRSA's Health Workforce Simulation Model (HWSM).[1] Supply projections are not included

---

* This is an edited, reformatted and augmented version of a fact sheet issued by the U.S. Department of Health and Human Services, Health Resources and Services Administration, April 2015.

due to lack of sufficient data to provide reliable estimates of future supply. Occupations discussed in this fact sheet include nuclear medicine technologists, radiologic technologists, diagnostic medical sonographers, medical and clinical laboratory technologists, and medical and clinical laboratory technicians. While the nuances of modeling supply and demand differ for individual health professions, within the HWSM the basic framework remains the same. The HWSM assumes that demand equals supply in the base year. For demand modeling, the major components include population demographics, health care use patterns (including the influence of the Affordable Care Act health care coverage), and demand for health care providers (translated into Full-Time Equivalents). Over the period studied, the model assumes that current national patterns of service demand remain unchanged within each demographic group.[2] These projections do not account for the geographical distribution of providers which may impact access to care in certain communities.

Background

The five technologist and technician occupations discussed in this brief fall into two categories: *diagnostic imaging providers* and *diagnostic medical laboratory providers*. The diagnostic imaging occupations include nuclear medicine technologists, radiologic technologists, and diagnostic medical sonographers. Nuclear medicine technologists prepare and administer radioactive drugs to patients undergoing nuclear medicine imaging scans. They operate special imaging equipment that detects and visualizes abnormalities in the body where the radioactive drugs concentrate. Nuclear medicine technologists must have a certificate, associate's, or bachelor's degree education. Requirements for licensure vary by state. Radiologic technologists perform diagnostic imaging procedures including X-rays, mammography, magnetic resonance imaging (MRI), and computed tomography (CT) for interpretation by radiology physicians. Radiologic technologists are most commonly educated in associate degree programs, and must be licensed or certified in some states. Diagnostic medical sonographers use high frequency sound waves (ultrasound) to produce images of internal organs for diagnosis and interpretation by a physician. Sonographers must have a postsecondary certificate or associate degree, and many employers require certification.

The diagnostic laboratory services occupations reported in this fact sheet include medical and clinical laboratory technologists and technicians. Both medical laboratory technologists and technicians collect samples and perform tests to analyze body fluids, tissue, and other substances. Technicians usually work under the general supervision of technologists or laboratory managers. Becoming a medical laboratory technologist typically requires a bachelor's degree. To become a medical laboratory technician, an associate's degree or certificate is required. Some states require laboratory personnel to be licensed or registered. To be licensed, a technologist often needs a bachelor's degree and must pass an exam. Certification of medical laboratory technologists and technicians is also required for licensure in some states and by some employers.

FINDINGS

There were approximately 20,900 nuclear medicine technologists, 194,800 radiologic technologists, and 58,000 diagnostic medical sonographers nationally in 2012. Demand for nuclear medicine technologists and radiologic technologists is projected to grow 24 percent between 2012 and 2025 (Exhibit 1). Demand for diagnostic medical sonographers is projected to increase by 21 percent during this same time period.

There were approximately 164,300 medical laboratory technologists and 161,500 medical laboratory technicians nationally in 2012. Between 2012 and 2025, demand for medical and clinical laboratory technologists and technicians is projected to grow by 22 percent for each occupation. For both technologists and technicians, 20 percent of this demand growth is associated with changing demographics. The aging of the population will lead to a greater need to diagnose medical conditions through laboratory procedures. The remaining 2 percent of the growth is associated with expanded insurance coverage under the Affordable Care Act. Collectively, the analysis presented here suggests that the U.S. will experience an increased demand for all five of these health technologist and technician occupations by 2025.

Exhibit 1. Estimated Demand for Selected Health Technologists and Technicians in the U.S., 2012 – 2025

	Nuclear medicine technologists	Radiologic technologists	Diagnostic medical sonographers	Medical and clinical laboratory technologists	Medical and clinical laboratory technicians
Demand					
Estimated demand, 2012	20,900	194,800	58,000	164,300	161,500
Total demand growth, 2012-2025:	5,000 (24%)	46,600 (24%)	12,200 (21%)	36,100 (22%)	35,400 (22%)
Changing demographics Impact	4,100	37,800	11,100	33,600	33,000
ACA insurance coverage Impact	900	8,800	1,100	2,500	2,400
Projected demand, 2025	25,900	241,400	70,200	200,400	196,900

End Notes

[1] This model uses a micro-simulation approach where supply is projected based on the simulation of career choices of individual health workers. Demand for health care services is simulated for a representative sample of the current and future U.S. population based on each person's demographic and socioeconomic characteristics, health-related behavior, and health risk factors that affect their health care utilization patterns. For more information on data and methods, please see Health Workforce Supply and Demand Simulation Model.

[2] Ono T, Lafortune G, Schoenstein M. "Health workforce planning in OECD countries: a review of 26 projection models from 18 countries." OECD Health Working Papers, No. 62. France: OECD Publishing; 2013:8-11.

In: U.S. Health Care Workforce
Editor: Sheldon T. Barrett

ISBN: 978-1-63485-730-7

Chapter 6

HEALTH WORKFORCE PROJECTIONS: PHARMACISTS*

National Center for Health Workforce Analysis

KEY FINDINGS

Between 2012 and 2025:

- The pharmacist supply is projected to grow by 35 percent.
- The demand for pharmacists is projected to grow by 16 percent.

This fact sheet presents the national supply of and demand for pharmacists for 2012 through 2025 using HRSA's Health Workforce Simulation Model (HWSM).[1] While the nuances of modeling supply and demand differ for individual health professions, the basic framework remains the same. The HWSM assumes that demand equals supply in the base year. For supply modeling, the major components (beyond common labor-market factors like unemployment) include characteristics of the existing workforce in a given occupation, new entrants to the workforce (e.g., newly trained workers), and workforce decisions (e.g., retirement and hours worked patterns). For demand modeling, the major components include population demographics, health care

* This is an edited, reformatted and augmented version of a fact sheet issued by the U.S. Department of Health and Human Services, Health Resources and Services Administration, December 2014.

use patterns (including the influence of the Affordable Care Act insurance coverage), and demand for prescription medications (translated into requirements for Full-Time Equivalents). Over the period studied, the model assumes that current national patterns of labor supply and service demand remain unchanged within each demographic group. [2] These projections do not account for the geographical distribution of providers which may impact access to care in certain areas/communities.

BACKGROUND

Pharmacists are licensed health care providers, with new entrants prepared at the doctoral level. [3] Pharmacists manage the dispensing of medications to patients and provide patient education to ensure their safe use. In many states, pharmacists are also able to provide routine immunizations for patients. In a few states, further training and certification allows for additional advanced practice roles for clinical pharmacists.[4]

FINDINGS

The supply of pharmacists is projected to increase by 35 percent between 2012 and 2025 (Exhibit 1), reflecting growth over the past decade in the annual number of new pharmacists trained. Demand for pharmacists, which is determined by the number of prescriptions filled, is projected to grow by 16 percent. It is projected that supply will exceed demand in 2025, suggesting that the U.S. will have adequate numbers of pharmacists to meet future demand.

Projections from the HWSM account for the implementation of the Affordable Care Act, and the resulting increase in the number of Americans with health insurance and prescription drug coverage.

There are some factors that will affect future demand but could not be accounted for in this forecasting model. For example, changes in reimbursement could incentivize pharmacists to provide extended counseling and other clinical services to patients, requiring more pharmacists to meet patient demand. The eventual elimination of the coverage gap for prescription drugs in Medicare Part D will also have a direct impact on the use of pharmaceutical services as greater access to prescription drug coverage will likely improve medication compliance and increase the demand for pharmacy professionals.[5] Additional demand may also be seen from the increasing integration of clinical pharmacists onto medical teams in settings such as patient-centered medical homes, and into other more advanced clinical roles.[6]

Exhibit 1. Estimated Supply and Demand for Pharmacists in the U.S., 2012 ± 2025

	Pharmacists
Supply	
Estimated supply, 2012	264,100
Total supply growth, 2012-2025:	91,200 (35%)
New entrants	160,500
Changing work patterns (e.g., part time to full time hours)	(7,960)
Attrition (e.g., retirements, mortality)	(61,340)
Projected supply, 2025	355,300
Demand	
Estimated demand, 2012	264,100
Total demand growth, 2012-2025:	42,300 (16%)
Changing demographics impact	35,800 (14%)
ACA insurance coverage impact	6,500 (2%)
Projected demand, 2025	306,400
Adequacy of supply, 2025	
Projected supply (minus) projected demand	48,900

End Notes

[1] This model uses a micro-simulation approach where supply is projected based on the simulation of career choices of individual health workers. Demand for health care services is simulated for a representative sample of the current and future U.S. population based on each person's demographic and socioeconomic characteristics, health-related behavior, and health risk factors that affect their health care utilization patterns. For more information on data and methods, please see http://bhw.hrsa.gov/healthworkforce/supplydemand/simulationmodel documentation.pdf.

[2] Ono T, Lafortune G, Schoenstein M. "Health workforce planning in OECD countries: a review of 26 projection models from 18 countries." OECD Health Working Papers, No. 62. France: OECD Publishing; 2013:8-11.

[3] A requirement since 2006, a large percentage of the existing workforce does not hold a PharmD degree. Pharmacy Manpower Project (PMP), Inc. 2009 National Pharmacist Workforce Survey. Alexandria, Virginia, USA: Downloaded from: http://www.pharmacy.wsu.edu/ information/2009.Pharmacist.Workforce.Survey.pdf.

[4] "About Clincial Pharmacists." American College of Clinical Pharmacy. n.d, Downloaded from: http://www.accp.com/about/clinicalpharmacists.aspx.

[5] USA Pharmacist, Affordable Care Act Mostly Upheld. 2012. See: http://www.uspharmacist.com/content/d/pharmacy law/c/36134/.

[6] Scott MA, Hitch B, Ray L, Colvin G. 3Integration of pharmacists into a patient-centered medical home.´ Journal of the American Pharmacy Association (2003). 2011 Mar-Apr; 51(2):161-6.

In: U.S. Health Care Workforce
Editor: Sheldon T. Barrett
ISBN: 978-1-63485-730-7

Chapter 7

Health Workforce Projections: Occupational Therapy and Physical Therapy*

National Center for Health Workforce Analysis

Key Findings

Between 2012 and 2025:

- Supply is estimated to grow by 46 p ercent for occupational therapists and 33 percent for physicaltherapists.
- Demand is estimated to grow by 20 percent for occupational therapists and 23 percent for physicaltherapists.
- The projected supply of individuals in each occupation exceeds the projected growth in service demand for occupational therapists and physical therapists.

This fact sheet presents the national supply and demand for occupational and physical therapists between 2012 and 2025 using HRSA's Health Workforce Simulation Model (HWSM).[1] While the nuances of modeling

* This is an edited, reformatted and augmented version of a fact sheet issued by the U.S. Department of Health and Human Services, Health Resources and Services Administration, December 2014.

supply and demand differ for individual health professions, the basic framework remains the same. The HWSM assumes that demand equals supply in the base year. For supply modeling, the major components (beyond common labor-market factors like unemployment) include characteristics of the existing workforce in a given occupation, new entrants to the workforce (e.g., newly trained workers), and workforce decisions (e.g., retirement and hours worked patterns). For demand modeling, the major components include population demographics, health care use patterns (including the influence of the Affordable Care Act insurance coverage), and demand for health care services (translated into requirements for Full-Time Equivalents). Over the period studied, the model assumes that current national patterns of labor supply and service demand remain unchanged within each demographic group.[2] These projections do not account for the geographical distribution of providers which may impact access to care in certain areas/communities.

BACKGROUND

Occupational therapy is a health, wellness, and rehabilitation profession that helps individuals maximize their performance and functioning throughout the lifespan. Occupational therapists are prepared at the Master's or Doctoral level. They assess and treat people who are injured, ill, or disabled and help them to recover, improve, and develop skills needed for daily living and working. Examples of common occupational therapy interventions include: helping people recovering from strokes to regain life skills, supporting elderly individuals with cognitive-behavioral or physical impairments to improve their functionality, and helping children born with disabilities to fully participate in daily activities.

Physical therapists are professionals providing rehabilitation, habilitation, preventive, and risk reduction services for patients. New physical therapists are now prepared at the doctoral level. Physical therapists help assess, maintain, restore, and improve movement, activity, and health to enable individuals to enjoy optimal physical function.

FINDINGS

Between 2012 and 2025, supply is estimated to grow by 46 percent for occupational therapists and 33 percent for physical therapists (Exhibit 1). The demand for occupational therapists is projected to grow by 20 percent and demand for physical therapists is projected to grow by 23 percent. Thus, the projected growth in supply exceeds the projected growth in demand for services for both occupational therapists and physical therapists. These projections suggest that the U.S. should have a more than sufficient supply of occupational therapists and physical therapists to meet the projected growth in demand for services by 2025.

Exhibit 1. Estimated Supply and Demand for Rehabilitation/Habilitation Services in the U.S., 2012-2025

	Occupational therapists	*Physical therapists*
Supply		
Estimated supply, 2012	86,300	191,600
Total supply growth, 2012-2025:	39,900 (46%)	62,600 (33%)
New entrants	58,200	96,500
Changing work patterns(e.g., part time to full time hours)	(2,510)	(1,030)
Attrition (e.g., retirements, mortality)	(15,790)	(32,870)
Projected supply, 2025	126,200	254,200
Demand		
Estimated demand, 2012	86,300	191,600
Total demand growth, 2012-2025	17,600 (20%)	43,500 (23%)
Changing demographics impact	17,200 (20%)	40,800 (21%)
ACA insurance coverage impact	400 (0%)	2,700 (1%)
Projected demand, 2025	103,900	235,100
Adequacy of supply, 2025		
Projected supply (minus) projected demand	22,300	19,100

Several factors that influence demand are included in the HWSM. The aging and growth of the U.S. population, the Affordable Care Act's emphasis on wellness and prevention, and current initiatives to better manage chronic illness—including diabetes and heart disease—suggest that demand for occupational and physical therapy services will remain high, and were factored into the projections discussed here. A limitation of the model is that it does not account for other factors that might influence demand, such as the increasing recognition of the needs of disabled Americans, including veterans and those returning from foreign wars.

End Notes

[1] This model uses a micro-simulation approach where supply is projected based on the simulation of career choices of individual health workers. Demand for health Ono T, Lafortune G, Schoenstein M. "Health workforce planning in OECD countries: a review of 26 projection models from 18 countries." OECD Health Working Papers, No. 62. France: OECD Publishing; 2013:8-11.

[2] care services is simulated for a representative sample of the current and future U.S. population based on each person's demographic and socioeconomic characteristics, health-related behavior, and health risk factors that affect their health care utilization patterns. For more information on data and methods, please see http://bhw.hrsa.gov/healthworkforce/supplydemand/simulationmodeldocumentation.pdf.

In: U.S. Health Care Workforce
Editor: Sheldon T. Barrett
ISBN: 978-1-63485-730-7

Chapter 8

HEALTH WORKFORCE PROJECTIONS: VISION OCCUPATIONS*

National Center for Health Workforce Analysis

KEY FINDINGS

Between 2012 and 2025:

- The supply of optometrists is projected to grow by 21 percent.
- The supply of opticians is projected to decrease by 6 percent; however this may be due to the model's inability to account for on-the-job training.
- The demand for both optometrists and opticians is projected to grow by 15 percent.

This fact sheet presents the national supply and demand for optometrists and opticians between 2012 and 2025 using HRSA's Health Workforce Simulation Model (HWSM).[1] While the nuances of modeling supply and demand differ for individual health professions, the basic framework remains the same. The HWSM assumes that demand equals supply in the base year. For supply modeling, the major components (beyond common labor-market

---

* This is an edited, reformatted and augmented version of a fact sheet issued by the U.S. Department of Health and Human Services, Health Resources and Services Administration, December 2014.

factors like unemployment) include characteristics of the existing workforce in a given occupation, new entrants to the workforce (e.g., newly trained workers), and workforce decisions (e.g., retirement and hours worked patterns). For demand modeling, the major components include population demographics, health care use patterns (including the influence of Affordable Care Act insurance coverage), and demand for health care services (translated into requirements for Full-Time Equivalents). Over the period studied, the model assumes that current national patterns of labor supply and service demand remain unchanged within each demographic group.[2] These projections do not account for the geographical distribution of providers which may impact access to care in certain areas/communities.

BACKGROUND

Optometrists perform eye exams and vision tests, in addition to diagnosing and treating visual problems, diseases, and injuries. They prescribe and dispense corrective lenses and prescribe medications for certain eye diseases. An optometrist receives a doctor of optometry (OD) degree after completing four years of optometry school, preceded by three or more years of college. They must be licensed to practice in a particular state.[3]

Following prescriptions from optometrists and ophthalmologists, dispensing opticians help fit eyeglasses and contact lenses. They also advise consumers regarding eyeglass frame or contact lens purchase options. Opticians typically have a high school diploma or equivalent and some form of on-the-job training. Some opticians enter the occupation with an associate's degree or a certificate from a community college or technical school. Licensure is required in some states.[4]

FINDINGS

Based on the current size of the workforce and the number of individuals training in this field, optometrist supply is projected to grow by 21 percent between 2012 and 2025. For opticians, however, the supply is expected to decrease by 6 percent during the same timeframe. This is likely due to the fact that the number of opticians receiving formal training (e.g., associate's degree or a college/technical school certificate) is relatively small, approximately 880 per year, and the model cannot account for the fact that many opticians enter the profession by receiving on-the-job training. Therefore, the supply projections here likely underestimate the future total supply of opticians.

Between 2012 and 2025, the demand for both optometrists and opticians is projected to grow by 15 percent. Several factors that influence demand are included in the HWSM. Growth in the elderly population is expected to increase demand for eye care services because the prevalence of vision problems increases with age. Increasing rates of chronic diseases such as diabetes may also increase the demand for optician's and optometrist's services. The Affordable Care Act provided some provisions for eye care coverage—with most associated with the vision needs of children. Examples of provisions include waiving costs for children's eye exams and providing coverage for one pair of eyeglasses per year.

Findings from the HWSM suggest that between 2012 and 2025 projected supply of optometrists will be adequate, whereas approximately 11,200 additional opticians will be needed from on-the-job training unless enrollments were doubled in formal training programs for opticians.

Exhibit 1. Estimated Supply and Demand for Vision Services in the U.S., 2012-2025

	Optometrists	Opticians
Supply		
Estimated supply, 2012	36,300	54,500
Total supply growth, 2012-2025:	7,500 (21%)	-3,200 (-6%)
New entrants	18,250	11,440
Changing work patterns (e.g., part time to full time hours)	(2,460)	830
Attrition (e.g., retirements, mortality)	(8,290)	(15,470)
Projected supply, 2025	43,800	51,300
Demand		
Estimated demand, 2012	36,300	54,500
Total demand growth, 2012-2025	5,300 (15%)	8,000 (15%)
Changing demographics impact	3,700 (10%)	5,600 (10%)
ACA insurance coverage impact	1,600 (4%)	2,400 (4%)
Projected demand, 2025	41,600	62,500
Adequacy of supply, 2025		
Projected supply (minus) projected demand	2,200	-11,200

End Notes

[1] This model uses a micro-simulation approach where supply is projected based on the simulation of career choices of individual health workers. Demand for health care services is simulated for a representative sample of the current and future U.S. population based on each person's demographic and socioeconomic characteristics, health-related behavior, and health risk factors that affect their health care utilization patterns. For more information on data and methods, please see http://bhw.hrsa.gov/healthworkforce/supplydemand/simulationmodel documentation.pdf.

[2] Ono T, Lafortune G, Schoenstein M. "Health workforce planning in OECD countries: a review of 26 projection models from 18 countries." OECD Health Working Papers, No. 62. France: OECD Publishing; 2013:8-11.

[3] Occupational Outlook Handbook. 2014. U.S Bureau of Labor Statistics, available at http:// www.bls.gov/ooh/healthcare/optometrists.htm

[4] Occupational Outlook Handbook. 2014. U.S Bureau of Labor Statistics, available at http:// www.bls.gov/ooh/healthcare/opticians-dispensing.htm.

In: U.S. Health Care Workforce
Editor: Sheldon T. Barrett

ISBN: 978-1-63485-730-7

Chapter 9

HEALTH WORKFORCE PROJECTIONS: RESPIRATORY THERAPISTS*

National Center for Health Workforce Analysis

KEY FINDINGS

Between 2012 and 2025:

- The respiratory therapist supply is projected to grow by 70 percent.
- The demand for respiratory therapists is projected to grow by 20 percent.

This fact sheet presents the national supply of and demand for respiratory therapists for 2012 through 2025 using HRSA's Health Workforce Simulation Model (HWSM).[1] While the nuances of modeling supply and demand differ for individual health professions, the basic framework remains the same. The HWSM assumes that demand equals supply in the base year. For supply modeling, the major components (beyond common labor-market factors such as unemployment) include characteristics of the existing workforce in a given occupation, new entrants to the workforce (e.g., newly trained workers), and workforce decisions (e.g., retirement and hours worked patterns). For demand

* This is an edited, reformatted and augmented version of a fact sheet issued by the U.S. Department of Health and Human Services, Health Resources and Services Administration, April 2015.

modeling, the major components include population demographics, health care use patterns (including the influence of the Affordable Care Act health care coverage), and demand for health care providers (translated into Full-Time Equivalents). Over the period studied, the model assumes that current national patterns of labor supplied and services demanded remain unchanged within each demographic group.[2] These projections do not account for the geographical distribution of providers which may impact access to care in certain communities.

BACKGROUND

Respiratory therapists care for patients with disorders affecting the cardiopulmonary system such as cardiovascular disease, pneumonia, and chronic respiratory disease (e.g., asthma or emphysema). They also provide emergency care to patients suffering from trauma, heart attacks, drowning, or shock. Respiratory therapists conduct a variety of patient evaluation and education activities. Those working in home care settings teach patients and their families to use ventilators and other life-support systems. In a hospital setting they perform a myriad of duties such as managing ventilators and artificial airway devices, testing patients' breathing capacity, and providing breathing treatments.

An associate's degree is the minimum educational requirement, with employers often preferring that applicants possessing a bachelor's degree or master's degree from a post-graduate program. Many colleges and universities, vocational–technical institutes, and the Armed Forces offer education and training programs which award an associate's or bachelor's degree. All programs have clinical components that allow therapists to earn course credit and gain supervised experience treating patients.

Respiratory therapists are licensed in all states except Alaska. Although varying by state, licensure requirements in most states include completing a state or professional certification exam.

FINDINGS

Analysis of the American Community Survey data suggests that in 2012 there were approximately 104,100 active respiratory therapists in the U.S. The majority of respiratory therapists are employed in hospitals. Other employment settings include nursing care facilities and home care.

The supply of respiratory therapists is projected to increase by 70 percent between 2012 and 2025 (Exhibit 1). Demand for respiratory therapists is projected to grow by 20 percent. It is projected that supply will exceed demand in 2025, suggesting that the U.S. will have more than adequate numbers of respiratory therapists to meet future demand.

Exhibit 1. Estimated Supply and Demand for Respiratory Therapists in the U.S., 2012 – 2025

	Respiratory Therapists
Supply	
Estimated supply, 2012	104,100
Total supply growth, 2012-2025:	73,100 (70%)
New entrants	105,510
Changing work patterns (e.g., part time to full time hours)	(5,720)
Attrition (e.g., retirements, mortality)	(26,690)
Projected supply, 2025	177,200
Demand	
Estimated demand, 2012	104,100
Total demand growth, 2012-2025:	21,200 (20%)
Changing demographics impact	19,500
ACA insurance coverage impact	1,700
Projected demand, 2025	125,300
Adequacy of supply, 2025	
Projected supply (minus) projected demand	51,900

Future growth of the nation's elderly population, which is accounted for in the HWSM, will likely lead to increased incidence of respiratory conditions that can permanently damage the lungs or restrict lung function. This growing disease burden will lead to an increased demand for respiratory therapy services and treatments, primarily in hospital and nursing home settings.

End Notes

[1] This model uses a micro-simulation approach where supply is projected based on the simulation of career choices of individual health workers. Demand for health care services is simulated for a representative sample of the current and future U.S. population based on each person's

demographic and socioeconomic characteristics, health-related behavior, and health risk factors that affect their health care utilization patterns. For more information on data and methods, please see BHW HRSA Health Workforce Supply and Demand.

[2] Ono T, Lafortune G, Schoenstein M. "Health workforce planning in OECD countries: a review of 26 projection models from 18 countries." OECD Health Working Papers, No. 62. France: OECD Publishing; 2013:8-11.

In: U.S. Health Care Workforce
Editor: Sheldon T. Barrett
ISBN: 978-1-63485-730-7

Chapter 10

HEALTH WORKFORCE PROJECTIONS: CHIROPRACTORS AND PODIATRISTS*

National Center for Health Workforce Analysis

KEY FINDINGS

Between 2012 and 2025:

- Supply is estimated to grow by 30 percent for chiropractors and 36 percent for podiatrists.
- Demand is estimated to grow by 16 percent for chiropractors and 22 percent for podiatrists.
- The projected supply of individuals in each occupation exceeds the projected growth in service demand for chiropractors and podiatrists.

This fact sheet presents the national supply of and demand for chiropractors and podiatrists for 2012 through 2025 using HRSA's Health Workforce Simulation Model (HWSM).[1] While the nuances of modeling supply and demand differ for individual health professions, the basic framework remains the same. The HWSM assumes that demand equals supply in the base year. For supply modeling, the major components (beyond

* This is an edited, reformatted and augmented version of a fact sheet issued by the U.S. Department of Health and Human Services, Health Resources and Services Administration, April 2015.

common labor-market factors such as unemployment) include characteristics of the existing workforce in a given occupation, new entrants to the workforce (e.g., newly trained workers), and workforce decisions (e.g., retirement and hours worked patterns). For demand modeling, the major components include population demographics, health care use patterns (including the influence of the Affordable Care Act health care coverage), and demand for health care providers (translated into Full-Time Equivalents). Over the period studied, the model assumes that current national patterns of labor supply and service demand remain unchanged within each demographic group.[2] These projections do not account for the geographical distribution of providers which may impact access to care in certain communities.

BACKGROUND

Chiropractors care for patients with health problems in their neuromusculoskeletal system using spinal adjustments, manipulation, manual therapy, and other techniques. Chiropractors are required to have a Doctor of Chiropractic (D.C.) degree, a post-graduate degree that typically takes 4 years to complete. In 2012, there were 15 Doctor of Chiropractic programs accredited by The Council on Chiropractic Education. Following graduation, some chiropractors complete postgraduate programs in specialty areas, such as orthopedics and pediatrics that lead to certification. Although specific requirements vary by state, all states require chiropractors to be licensed.

Podiatrists provide medical and surgical care for people with foot, ankle, and lower leg problems. They diagnose illnesses, treat injuries, and perform surgery involving the lower extremities. Some podiatrists specialize in performing advanced surgeries, such as foot and ankle reconstruction. Others choose specialties such as sports medicine or pediatrics. Podiatrists must have a Doctor of Podiatric Medicine (DPM) degree from an accredited college of podiatric medicine. A DPM degree program takes 4 years to complete. In 2012, there were nine colleges of podiatric medicine accredited by the Council on Podiatric Medical Education. After earning a DPM, podiatrists must complete a podiatric medical and surgical residency (PMSR) program. Podiatrists in every state must also be licensed.

FINDINGS

Between 2012 and 2025, supply is estimated to grow by 30 percent for chiropractors and 36 percent for podiatrists (Exhibit 1). The demand for chiropractors is projected to grow by 16 percent and demand for podiatrists is projected to grow by 22 percent. Thus, the projected growth in supply exceeds the projected growth in demand for services for both chiropractors and podiatrists. These projections suggest that the U.S. should have a sufficient supply of chiropractors and podiatrists to meet the projected growth in demand for services by 2025.

Exhibit 1. Estimated Supply and Demand for Chiropractors and Podiatrists in the U.S., 2012 – 2025

	Chiropractors	Podiatrists
Supply		
Estimated supply, 2012	58,800	10,700
Total supply growth, 2012-2025:	17,500 (30%)	3,900 (36%)
New entrants	33,810	6,980
Changing work patterns (e.g., part time to full time hours)	(480)	250
Attrition (e.g., retirements, mortality)	(15,830)	(3,330)
Projected supply, 2025	76,300	14,600
Demand		
Estimated demand, 2012	58,800	10,700
Total demand growth, 2012-2025:	9,400 (16%)	2,400(22%)
Changing demographics impact	7,300	1,800
ACA insurance coverage impact	2,100	600
Projected demand, 2025	68,200	13,100
Adequacy of supply, 2025		
Projected supply (minus) projected demand	8,100	1,500

Projections from the HWSM account for the aging of the population and increased number of Americans with health insurance as a result of the Affordable Care Act implementation. The aging of the large baby-boom generation will likely lead to new opportunities for chiropractors, as most insurance plans now cover chiropractic services. Also due to population aging and growing rates of chronic conditions such as diabetes and obesity, the number of people expected to have mobility and foot-related problems will rise. These factors together with projected growth in services provided in outpatient surgery settings will create new future opportunities for podiatrists.

End Notes

[1] This model uses a micro-simulation approach where supply is projected based on the simulation of career choices of individual health workers. Demand for health care services is simulated for a representative sample of the current and future U.S. population based on each person's demographic and socioeconomic characteristics, health-related behavior, and health risk factors that affect their health care utilization patterns. For more information on data and methods, please see BHW HRSA Health Workforce Supply and Demand Simulation Model.

[2] Ono T, Lafortune G, Schoenstein M. "Health workforce planning in OECD countries: a review of 26 projection models from 18 countries." OECD Health Working Papers, No. 62. France: OECD Publishing; 2013:8-11.

In: U.S. Health Care Workforce
Editor: Sheldon T. Barrett

ISBN: 978-1-63485-730-7

Chapter 11

HEALTH WORKFORCE PROJECTIONS: DIETITIANS AND NUTRITIONISTS*

National Center for Health Workforce Analysis

KEY FINDINGS

Between 2012 and 2025:

- The dietitians and nutritionists supply is projected to grow by 36 percent.
- The demand for dietitians and nutritionists is projected to grow by 20 percent.

This fact sheet presents the national supply of and demand for dietitians and nutritionists for 2012 through 2025 using HRSA's Health Workforce Simulation Model (HWSM).[1] While the nuances of modeling supply and demand differ for individual health professions, the basic framework remains the same. The HWSM assumes that demand equals supply in the base year. For supply modeling, the major components (beyond common labor-market factors such as unemployment) include characteristics of the existing workforce in a given occupation, new entrants to the workforce (e.g., newly

* This is an edited, reformatted and augmented version of a fact sheet issued by the U.S. Department of Health and Human Services, Health Resources and Services Administration, April 2015.

trained workers), and workforce decisions (e.g., retirement and hours worked patterns). For demand modeling, the major components include population demographics, health care use patterns (including the influence of the Affordable Care Act health care coverage), and demand for health care providers (translated into Full-Time Equivalents). Over the period studied, the model assumes that current national patterns of labor supplied and services demanded remain unchanged within each demographic group.[2] These projections do not account for the geographical distribution of providers which may impact access to care in certain communities.

BACKGROUND

Dietitians and nutritionists advise people on the proper nutrition necessary to lead a healthy lifestyle or achieve a specific health-related goal. They have several specialty roles which include: providing medical nutrition therapy, developing programs and educating the public on food and nutrition topics, and planning meal programs in food service settings (e.g., hospitals, prisons, cafeterias, etc.). They also may work with other health care professionals using a team-based approach to coordinate patient care.

Although these two professions are related, they maintain some distinctive qualities. The biggest difference between dietitians and nutritionists lies in their licensure and educational pathways. Many dietitians choose to earn the Registered Dietitian Nutritionist (RDN) credential. RDNs are required to obtain at least a baccalaureate degree. While there are no formal educational requirements for nutritionists, many complete some formal coursework in nutrition-related subjects to qualify for employment. Nutritionists that choose to earn the Certified Nutrition Specialist (CNS) credential are required to complete a baccalaureate or advanced degree in a nutrition discipline.

FINDINGS

Between 2012 and 2025, the supply of dieticians and nutritionists is projected to increase by 36 percent (Exhibit 1), reflecting growth over the past decade in the annual number of new dieticians and nutritionists trained. Demand for dietitians and nutritionists is projected to grow by 20 percent. It is projected that supply will exceed demand in 2025, suggesting that the U.S.

will have adequate numbers of dieticians and nutritionists to meet future demand.

Exhibit 1. Estimated Supply and Demand for Dietitians and Nutritionists in the U.S., 2012 – 2025

	Dietitians and Nutritionists
Supply	
Estimated supply, 2012	67,400
Total supply growth, 2012-2025:	24,000 (36%)
New entrants	*45,840*
Changing work patterns (e.g., part time to full time hours)	*1,280*
Attrition (e.g., retirements, mortality)	*(23,120)*
Projected supply, 2025	91,400
Demand	
Estimated demand, 2012	67,400
Total demand growth, 2012-2025:	13,600 (20%)
Changing demographics impact	*13,000*
ACA insurance coverage impact	*600*
Projected demand, 2025	81,000
Adequacy of supply, 2025	
Projected supply (minus) projected demand	10,400

The HWSM accounts for the aging of the population, which will result in an increase in chronic conditions and the associated demand for dietetic services. However, with high rates of obesity and metabolic disease across the U.S. and national goals to reduce prevalence of these conditions, growth in demand for dieticians and nutritionists could be higher than projected under the scenario modeled.

End Notes

[1] This model uses a micro-simulation approach where supply is projected based on the simulation of career choices of individual health workers. Demand for health care services is simulated for a representative sample of the current and future U.S. population based on each person's demographic and socioeconomic characteristics, health-related behavior, and health risk factors that affect their health care utilization patterns. For more information on data and

methods, please see BHW HRSA Health Workforce Supply and Demand Stimulation Model.

[2] Ono T, Lafortune G, Schoenstein M. "Health workforce planning in OECD countries: a review of 26 projection models from 18 countries." OECD Health Working Papers, No. 62. France: OECD Publishing; 2013:8-11.

In: U.S. Health Care Workforce
Editor: Sheldon T. Barrett

ISBN: 978-1-63485-730-7

Chapter 12

HEALTH WORKFORCE PROJECTIONS: PSYCHOLOGISTS*

National Center for Health Workforce Analysis

KEY FINDINGS

Between 2012 and 2025:

- The psychologist supply is projected to decline by 900 psychologists.
- The demand for psychologists is projected to grow by 10 percent.

This fact sheet presents the national supply of and demand for psychologists for 2012 through 2025 using HRSA's Health Workforce Simulation Model (HWSM).[1] While the nuances of modeling supply and demand differ for individual health professions, the basic framework remains the same. The HWSM assumes that demand equals supply in the base year. For supply modeling, the major components (beyond common labor-market factors such as unemployment) include characteristics of the existing workforce in a given occupation, new entrants to the workforce (e.g., newly trained workers), and workforce decisions (e.g., retirement and hours worked patterns). For demand modeling, the major components include population

* This is an edited, reformatted and augmented version of a fact sheet issued by the U.S. Department of Health and Human Services, Health Resources and Services Administration, April 2015.

demographics, health care use patterns (including the influence of the Affordable Care Act health care coverage), and demand for health care providers (translated into Full-Time Equivalents). Over the period studied, the model assumes that current national patterns of labor supplied and services demanded remain unchanged within each demographic group.[2] These projections do not account for the geographical distribution of providers which may impact access to care in certain communities.

BACKGROUND

Psychologists traditionally treat patients with mental and emotional problems, but they also serve as scientists researching the phenomenon of human behavior. In particular, they concentrate on behaviors that affect the mental and emotional health, and mental functioning of people. A doctoral degree is typically required for most clinical, counseling, and research psychologists. Although licensing laws for psychologists vary by state and type of position, most states require some form of licensure or certification. All states require psychologists who practice independently to be licensed. Psychologists' typical employment settings include clinics, hospitals, rehabilitation facilities, and community and mental health centers.

FINDINGS

Analysis of the American Community Survey data suggests approximately 188,300 psychologists were in active practice in 2012, with nearly one-third self-employed. About a third (31 percent) worked in educational services, and about 30 percent worked in health care and social assistance.

Between 2012 and 2025, the supply of psychologists appears to be declining slightly by about 900 individuals (Exhibit 1).

Between 2012 and 2025, the demand for psychologists is projected to grow by 10 percent. Demand for psychologists in health care is expected to increase as behavioral and mental health is increasingly integrated with primary care. Historically, many health insurance plans have provided less coverage for mental health services compared to physical health services. The Affordable Care Act includes mental health and substance abuse treatment among its 10 "essential" benefits, which means that health plans offered in the individual and small group markets, both inside and outside of the Health Insurance Marketplace, must offer a comprehensive package of items and services which may further increase demand for services. This is accounted for in estimates shown above. The estimates do not account for the movement in the health care system towards more integrated care, where primary care providers work in team settings with psychiatrists, social workers and other mental health care professionals to provide comprehensive, interdisciplinary care, including treating mental and behavioral health issues.[3] Findings from the HWSM suggest that between 2012 and 2025 the nation's projected supply of psychologists will fall short of demand.

Exhibit 1. Estimated Supply and Demand for Psychologists in the U.S., 2012 – 2025

	Psychologists
Supply	
Estimated supply, 2012	188,300
Total supply growth, 2012-2025:	(900) (0%)
New entrants	*74,670*
Changing work patterns (e.g., part time to full time hours)	*(1,810)*
Attrition (e.g., retirements, mortality)	*(73,760)*
Projected supply, 2025	187,400
Demand	
Estimated demand, 2012	188,300
Total demand growth, 2012-2025:	19,700
Changing demographics impact	*17,300*
ACA insurance coverage impact	*2,400*
Projected demand, 2025	208,000
Adequacy of supply, 2025	
Projected supply (minus) projected demand	(20,600)

End Notes

[1] This model uses a micro-simulation approach where supply is projected based on the simulation of career choices of individual health workers. Demand for health care services is simulated for a representative sample of the current and future U.S. population based on each person's demographic and socioeconomic characteristics, health-related behavior, and health risk factors that affect their health care utilization patterns. For more information on data and methods, please see BHW HRSA Health Workforce Supply and Demand Simulation Model.

[2] Ono T, Lafortune G, Schoenstein M. "Health workforce planning in OECD countries: a review of 26 projection models from 18 countries." OECD Health Working Papers, No. 62. France: OECD Publishing; 2013:8-11.

[3] SAMHSA Primary care in behavioral health: primary and behavioral health care integration grantees. Available at http://www.integration.samhsa.gov/integratedcare-models/primary-care-in-behavioral-health#pbhci grantees. Accessed February 2, 2015.

In: U.S. Health Care Workforce
Editor: Sheldon T. Barrett
ISBN: 978-1-63485-730-7

Chapter 13

HEALTH CARE WORKFORCE: COMPREHENSIVE PLANNING BY HHS NEEDED TO MEET NATIONAL NEEDS*

United States Government Accountability Office

WHY GAO DID THIS STUDY

An adequate, well-trained, and diverse health care workforce is essential for providing access to quality health care services. The federal government—largely through HHS—funds programs to help ensure a sufficient supply and distribution of health care professionals. Some experts suggest that maintaining access to care could require an increase in the supply of providers, while others suggest access can be maintained by, among other things, greater use of technology.

GAO was asked to review HHS's workforce efforts. In this report, GAO examines (1) HHS's planning efforts for ensuring an adequate supply and distribution of the nation's health care workforce and (2) the extent to which individual HHS health care workforce programs contribute to meeting national needs. GAO reviewed strategic planning documents, workforce projection reports, and other related documents obtained from HHS agencies; interviewed

* This is an edited, reformatted and augmented version of a United States Government Accountability Office, Publication No. GAO-16-17, dated December 2015.

HHS officials; and analyzed performance measures for the largest health care workforce programs operated by HHS.

WHAT GAO RECOMMENDS

GAO recommends that HHS develop a comprehensive and coordinated planning approach that includes performance measures, identifies any gaps between its workforce programs and national needs, and identifies actions to close these gaps. HHS concurred with GAO's recommendations and provided technical comments, which GAO incorporated as appropriate.

WHAT GAO FOUND

The Department of Health and Human Services (HHS) engages in some planning for the 72 health care workforce programs administered by its agencies, but lacks comprehensive planning and oversight to ensure that these efforts meet national health care workforce needs. HHS's current strategic plan includes broad strategies—such as improving access to comprehensive primary and preventive medical services in historically underserved areas and supporting federally funded health centers—to which department officials said the health care workforce programs relate. However, these strategies do not explicitly reference workforce issues or specify how these programs contribute towards HHS's current strategic goals and performance targets. The health care workforce performance measures tracked by HHS and its agencies are specific to individual workforce programs and do not fully assess the overall adequacy of the department's workforce efforts. The Office of the Secretary leads workforce planning efforts, but it does not have an ongoing formal effort to ensure that the workforce programs distributed across its different agencies are aligned with national needs. Multiple external stakeholders, such as the Institute of Medicine and the Council on Graduate Medical Education, have reported that graduate medical education (GME) funding lacks the oversight and infrastructure to track outcomes, reward performance, and respond to emerging workforce challenges and that a more coordinated effort could help to ensure an adequate supply and distribution of the health care workforce. Consistent with leading practices, a coordinated department-wide planning effort is important to ensure that these efforts are aligned and managed effectively to meet workforce needs.

While HHS's workforce programs support education and training for multiple health professions, its largest programs do not specifically target areas of workforce need, such as for primary care and rural providers. For example, its two Medicare GME programs accounted for about three-quarters of HHS's fiscal year 2014 obligations for health care workforce development. However, HHS cannot target existing Medicare GME program funds to projected workforce shortage areas because the programs were established by statute and funds are disbursed based on a statutory formula that is unrelated to projected workforce needs. HHS has limited legal authority to target certain existing programs to areas of emerging needs and has taken steps to do so within its existing authorities, such as the approval of certain demonstration projects to test new payment models for Medicaid GME funds. Further, the President's budget has proposed additional authorities that would allow HHS to implement new education and training programs and payment reforms intended to support primary care providers, but these authorities have not been enacted and officials did not know the extent to which they would be sufficient to address identified needs. External stakeholders have recommended additional reforms that would allow these programs to better targets areas of need. Without a comprehensive and coordinated planning approach, HHS cannot fully identify gaps and actions to address those gaps, including determining whether additional legislative proposals are needed to ensure that its programs fully meet workforce needs.

ABBREVIATIONS

AAMC	Association of American Medical Colleges
ACF	Administration for Children and Families
ASFR	Assistant Secretary for Financial Resources
ASPE	Assistant Secretary for Planning and Evaluation
CMS	Centers for Medicare and Medicaid Services
COGME	Council on Graduate Medical Education
GME	graduate medical education
GPRA	Government Performance and Results Act of 1993
GPRAMA	GPRA Modernization Act of 2010
HCERA	Health Care and Education Reconciliation Act of 2010
HHS	Department of Health and Human Services

HRSA	Health Resources and Services Administration
HIS	Indian Health Service
IOM	Institute of Medicine
MedPAC	Medicare Payment Advisory Commission
NHSC	National Health Service Corps
PPACA	Patient Protection and Affordable Care Act
SAMHSA	Substance Abuse and Mental Health Services Administration

* * *

December 11, 2015
The Honorable Ron Johnson
Chairman
Committee on Homeland Security and Governmental Affairs
United States Senate

The Honorable Lamar Alexander
Chairman
Committee on Health, Education,
Labor and Pensions United States Senate

The Honorable Michael Enzi
Chairman
Subcommittee on Primary Health and Retirement Security
Committee on Health, Education, Labor and Pensions
United States Senate

The Honorable Richard Burr
United States Senate

An adequate, well-trained, and diverse health care workforce is essential for providing Americans with access to quality health care services.[1] According to some studies, a growing demand for services, an aging population, population growth, and increased access to insurance resulting from the implementation of the Patient Protection and Affordable Care Act (PPACA) could result in provider shortages that could limit patient access to care.[2] In addition to current workforce shortages for primary care and in rural areas, according to federal projections, by 2025, there will be national or regional shortages in a number of health professions, such as dentistry, psychiatry, general surgery, and nursing. Some experts report that maintaining access to care could require an increased supply of providers, while others suggest that access can be improved through policy options.[3] For example, they note that access to care could be increased through greater use of technology, such as telemedicine; changing the mix of providers delivering care; and changing the pattern of practice, such as by providing more team-based care or by eliminating currently provided care that is either unnecessary or of limited value.[4]

The federal government—largely through the Department of Health and Human Services (HHS)—funds a large number of education and training programs to help ensure a sufficient supply and distribution of physicians, nurses, dentists, and other health care professionals who provide care directly to patients.[5] These programs are managed by multiple HHS component agencies,[6] but in fiscal year 2014 about 90 percent of funding came through the Centers for Medicare and Medicaid Services (CMS) for graduate medical education (GME) payments to hospitals and other institutions that train physician residents. Most of the remaining HHS workforce funding in 2014 was administered by the Health Resources and Services Administration (HRSA) and generally offers financial assistance to students or institutions to encourage students to train and work in specific needed professions and regions. PPACA expanded many of these programs, in addition to creating new ones to increase training in direct health care professions and care in rural areas.[7] Effective strategic planning and timely workforce projections are important mechanisms for HHS to manage its health care workforce programs, although we have previously found that HHS has faced certain challenges in this area.[8]

Given the increased demands facing the nation's health care workforce and the diversity of HHS's existing programs, you asked us to study HHS's activities to ensure that federal funding is aligned with the nation's health care needs. In this report, we examine the following:

1. HHS's planning efforts for ensuring an adequate supply and distribution of the nation's health care workforce; and
2. The extent to which individual HHS health care workforce programs contribute to meeting national health care workforce needs.

To examine HHS's planning efforts for ensuring an adequate supply and distribution of the nation's health care workforce, we analyzed current and past HHS and component agency documents that contain information on goals, objectives, strategies, and metrics related to health care workforce planning and development. Specifically, we reviewed the four most recent HHS strategic plans (covering the periods 2014-2018, 2010-2015, 2007- 2012, and 2004-2009), as well as the President's recent budget proposals for HHS and HHS's annual performance plans and reports—which include performance goals and measures—for fiscal years 2014, 2015, and 2016. We also reviewed the most recent strategic plan for each HHS agency responsible for health care workforce programs,[9] and we interviewed agency officials to determine how its health care workforce strategies are aligned with related strategies in the most recent HHS strategic plan. We also interviewed HHS officials to identify HHS's rationale for its current approach to strategic planning for the health care workforce. We evaluated HHS's strategic planning and other efforts against the GPRA Modernization Act of 2010 (GPRAMA),[10] as well as leading practices for strategic planning and performance measurement identified in prior GAO work.[11] Finally, we reviewed recently published reports by the Institute of Medicine (IOM) and other organizations that have examined HHS's health care workforce programs and made recommendations.

To examine the extent to which individual HHS health care workforce programs contribute to meeting national health care workforce needs, we identified a list of 72 HHS programs that provided funding for workforce development in fiscal year 2014.[12] For each of these 72 programs, HHS provided basic funding and performance information. From this listing, we selected the 12 programs with the highest obligations—ranging from $42 million to $8 billion—in fiscal year 2014. These 12 programs accounted for 96 percent of the total obligations of the 72 programs. Of these 12 programs, 7 are administered by HRSA, 4 are administered by CMS, and 1 is administered by the Administration for Children and Families (ACF).[13] (See app. I for a list of these 12 programs.) For each of these 12 programs we did the following:

- reviewed performance measures to determine how they contribute toward department and agency goals;
- reviewed documentation and interviewed responsible officials to determine how HHS monitors these programs and how the workforce programs align with HHS strategic planning goals;
- compared agency performance management practices to criteria from GPRAMA as well as leading practices identified in prior GAO work;
- examined the extent to which these programs meet identified areas of health care workforce need; to identify areas of need, we reviewed the

- The remaining agencies collectively managed 19 programs, accounting for about 1 percent of total HHS workforce funding. (See fig. 3.)

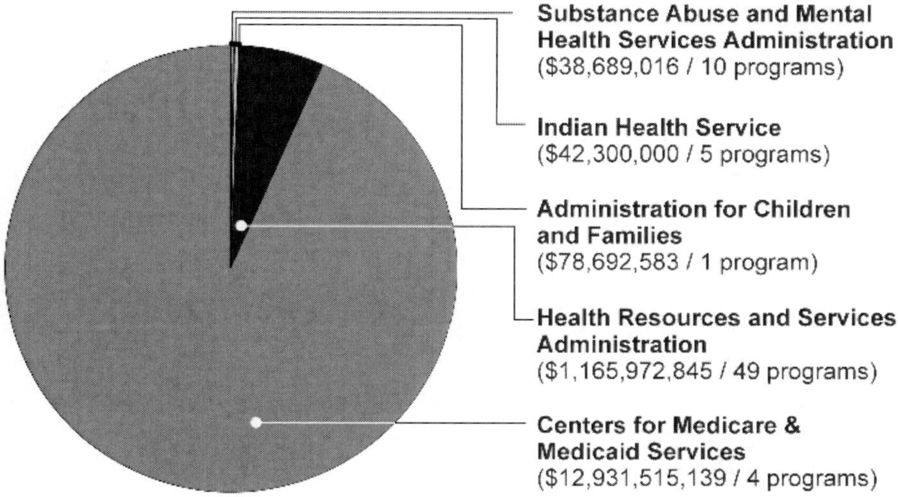

Source: GAO analysis of HHS data. | GAO-16-17.

Note: "Health care workforce" includes those professionals who provide direct health care, including, but not limited to, audiologists, chiropractors, dentists, medical assistants, nurses, occupational therapists, optometrists, pharmacists, physical therapists, physicians, physician assistants, podiatrists, psychologists, social workers, and counselors. The Office of the Surgeon General and the Office of Population Affairs collectively operate three additional health care workforce programs, obligating less than $5 million combined in fiscal year 2014.

Figure 3. HHS Obligations for Health Care Workforce Programs, by Agency, Fiscal Year 2014.

In addition to funding health care workforce programs, HHS examines information about the future demand for health care services, as well as the related supply and distribution of health professionals. Specifically, HRSA periodically publishes health care workforce projections regarding the supply and demand of the health care workforce.[18] We previously found that the agency's projections had not been updated and recommended that the agency develop a strategy and time frames to update national health care workforce projections regularly. Following that, HRSA awarded a contract to develop a new model, which according to officials has enabled more accurate estimates of workforce projections as well as workforce projections for a wider array of health professions.

The agency subsequently issued many of those projections later in 2014 and in 2015.[19]

HHS's Strategic Plan Lacks Specific Strategies for Its Health Care Workforce Programs Related to Their Effect on Access and Quality

HHS's current strategic plan lacks specificity regarding how health care workforce programs contribute to its strategic plan goals. Additionally, the performance targets that HHS publicly reports do not comprehensively assess the department's progress towards achieving its broader strategic plan goals regarding the health care workforce. Finally, the department engages in some coordinated planning, but lacks comprehensive planning and oversight to ensure that its many workforce efforts address identified national needs.

HHS Planning Efforts to Coordinate and Oversee Its Health Care Workforce Programs Do Not Ensure That National Needs Are Fully Addressed

HHS's strategic plan includes broad strategies to which the department's health care workforce efforts relate, but these strategies do not focus specifically on workforce issues. For example, the current 2014-2018 HHS strategic plan does not have a goal or objective specifically dedicated to health care workforce. Instead, HHS officials stated that workforce development efforts are distributed across various broad access and quality objectives within the plan's goal of strengthening health care.[20] Specifically, the plan includes seven strategies that contain a health care workforce component and that are distributed among three broad objectives. These strategies generally do not explicitly reference health care workforce training or education, but instead use broad statements that concurrently encompass numerous different components and methods for improving access to and quality of health care. For example, as part of one strategy, HHS seeks to improve access to comprehensive primary and preventative medical services in historically underserved areas and to support federally funded health centers. While not explicit in the plan, HHS officials indicated that developing the health care workforce is one element that contributes to these strategies. (See app. II for more details about the strategic plan.)

Past HHS strategic plans included more specific strategies and objectives related to the department's workforce programs. However, HHS officials told us that the department decided to remove most of workforce-specific language when developing the current plan. The prior HHS strategic plan (2010-2015) included a dedicated goal related to workforce development, with one objective and six corresponding strategies that were specific to health care workforce planning. Further, while an earlier HHS strategic plan (2007-2012) did not have a workforce-specific strategic goal, it also had one objective and corresponding strategies on health care workforce planning, similar to the detailed strategies in the 2010-2015 plan. However, HHS officials told us that in developing the current strategic plan, the department decided to remove most of the workforce-specific language because it determined that workforce development was an intermediate step in achieving the department's broader strategic goals of improving access to and quality of health care. They also noted that, due to the size of HHS—for fiscal year 2015, HHS spent over $1 trillion through its operating divisions—its strategic plan has to be high level and not too specific about any one topic.

Rather than include specificity in HHS's strategic plan, the department expects that the strategic plans of its agencies will contain additional detail about their health care workforce efforts, as is consistent with their mission, budget, and authorities. However, we found that these agency plans did not always contain this additional detail and were not always updated in a timely manner. For example, while HRSA's 2016-2018 strategic plan contains a dedicated health care workforce goal with three related objectives and eleven strategies, CMS's current 2013-2017 plan did not elaborate on any health care workforce issues presented in the HHS strategic plan, nor did it contain other related strategies. Moreover, IHS's strategic plan was last updated in 2006, and agency officials stated that the agency was not working to update the plan.[21] (See app. III for more details about agency strategic plans.) Consistent with GPRAMA leading practices, for strategic planning to achieve meaningful results on a crosscutting topic like workforce development, it is important that planning efforts across these agencies be coordinated with those of the department.[22]

In addition to developing its quadrennial strategic plans, HHS has previously developed other planning documents and workforce development efforts. For example, HHS has published a series of strategic initiatives outlining the Secretary's priorities. In 2014, one of these priorities was developing the health care workforce.[23] This document identified specific strategies for developing the health care workforce, such as targeting resources to areas of high need and strengthening the primary care workforce. The paper also discussed the need for reform to payment policy to better support emerging health care delivery models. However, as of November 2015, HHS had not released an update to this series of initiatives since the new Secretary assumed office in June 2014. In addition, previous presidential annual budgets have included proposals for improving HHS's health care workforce programs. Moreover, in conjunction with the President's fiscal year 2015 budget, HHS released a report in February 2014 providing additional information about the fiscal year 2015 proposals.[24] The report described the challenges to ensuring more diversity among and a better distribution of health care professionals and explained the costs and benefits associated with each of the proposals.

HHS Generally Assesses Progress of Individual Health Care Workforce Programs, But Lacks a Comprehensive Assessment of These Efforts Towards Achieving Broader Goals

HHS has identified a subset of performance measures that are intended to represent the effect that all existing health care workforce programs have on the department's broader goal of strengthening health care by improving access and quality. Among other places, HHS reports these workforce performance measures in its annual performance plan and report, which indicate progress towards achieving HHS strategic planning goals.[25] From fiscal year 2014 to 2016, the number of healthcare workforce performance measures tracked by HHS within its annual performance report dropped from five to two, and they are focused on a small percentage of programs.[26] Specifically, for fiscal year 2016, the two measures assess progress related to several HRSA programs— 4 National Health Service Corps (NHSC) programs and 14 Bureau of Health Workforce primary care training programs—that combined represent about 3 percent of the overall funding for all HHS health care workforce programs in fiscal year 2014. According to HHS officials, the department chooses not to include as part of the annual performance report all of the performance measures tracked by HHS agencies.[27] Officials said that these two measures were chosen to be tracked in the strategic plan and annual report because HHS identified them as part of a subset of measures that are representative of the department's overall programming efforts. However, these measures are specific to the 18 programs and do not fully assess the adequacy of the department's broader workforce efforts.

Moreover, HHS has no stated targets to assess the effectiveness of existing health care workforce programs on achieving the department's broader goal of strengthening health care by improving access and quality. As part of a larger measurement project, HHS tracks data on workforce that it indicates are closely related to the supply of trained health care providers. Specifically, HHS tracks (1) the percentage of individuals that have a usual source of medical care and (2) the number of primary care practitioners (such as physicians, nurse practitioners, and physician assistants). However, neither of these broad workforce indicators has a stated target related to necessary provider levels.[28]

GPRAMA leading practices indicate that for performance measures to be effective, agencies need to set specific targets. While it is important to have specific performance measures that assess individual programs, health care workforce is an issue that straddles many different programs and HHS agencies, and therefore it is also important to have broader measures that assess how these individual programs contribute to the department's overall effectiveness in developing the health care workforce to improve access to care. In the absence of these broader measures, HHS lacks information to help it comprehensively determine the extent to which programs are meeting the department's goal of strengthening health care or identify gaps between current health care workforce programs and unmet health care needs.

According to HHS, over three-quarters of the 72 health care workforce programs had performance measures tracked by the relevant HHS agency. HHS indicated that its smaller health care workforce programs generally had performance measures and targets. For example, HRSA's 7 largest health care workforce programs, which accounted for about 5 percent of HHS's health care workforce obligations in fiscal year 2014, each had related performance measures. For most of these 7 programs, HRSA reported meeting or exceeding its performance targets in fiscal year 2014. For example, according to HRSA, the NHSC and Advanced Nurse Education programs exceeded their performance targets for fiscal year 2014, and the Children's Hospital GME program met or exceeded its fiscal year 2014 performance targets. (See app. I for more information about the performance measures of the 12 largest health care workforce programs.)

However, HHS lacks performance measures related to workforce development for their largest programs.[29] Specifically, HHS's 2 largest health care workforce programs—the Medicare GME programs run by CMS, accounting for 77 percent of obligations in fiscal year 2014—did not have performance measures directly aligned with areas of health care workforce needs identified in HRSA's workforce projection reports.[30] According to HHS officials, the GME programs are not aligned with the workforce objectives in HHS's strategic plan. Leading practices identified in prior GAO work show that for individual programs to address strategic goals and objectives, it is important that the programs be aligned with these goals, and that these goals influence the daily operation of the programs.[31]

HHS Coordinates Some Health Care Workforce Planning, but Lacks Comprehensive and Ongoing Oversight to Ensure Needs Are Fully Addressed

HHS does not have a consistent and ongoing effort to coordinate all of the workforce planning efforts and resources that are distributed across the department's various offices and agencies. According to HHS officials, HHS delegates responsibility for many of its health care workforce planning efforts to its component agencies, based on each agency's mission and expertise.[32] These agencies also collaborate with each other occasionally on various health care workforce development efforts, such as projection reports and workforce programs.[33] Officials said that HHS's coordination of these efforts generally occurs during the department's larger planning and budget process.

Within the HHS Office of the Secretary, ASFR coordinates the annual budget development process, and ASPE coordinates the quadrennial strategic planning process, and, in doing so, both lead activities to include workforce development in these efforts. In addition, ASPE occasionally collaborates with HHS advisory bodies, such as COGME, supports research on the health care workforce, and periodically creates interagency workgroups to discuss specific priorities that support the development of its budget proposals. However, outside of the context of these strategic planning and budgetary processes, ASPE does not have an ongoing formal effort to coordinate the workforce planning efforts of HHS agencies. Additionally, it does not regularly monitor or facilitate HHS interagency collaborations on workforce efforts or fully communicate identified gaps to stakeholders. A separate entity within the Office of the Secretary, ASFR, coordinates the monitoring of those performance measures for health care workforce programs that the department tracks in its annual performance plan and report. Similar to ASPE, according to officials, ASFR engages in these coordinating and monitoring efforts primarily within the context of developing the annual performance report.

To achieve meaningful results, GPRAMA leading practices emphasize the importance of coordinating planning efforts across agencies and departments.[34] Leading practices state that when multiple federal programs that address a similar issue are spread over many agencies and departments, a coordinated planning approach is important to ensuring that efforts across multiple agencies are aligned.[35] Specifically, a coordinated planning approach is essential to (1) setting targets for these workforce programs and other efforts; (2) identifying and communicating whether there are gaps between existing workforce programs and future needs; and (3) determining whether agencies have the necessary information to assess the reach and effectiveness of their programs. While coordination at the program level is important, it does not take the place of, or achieve the level of, overall department coordination that we have previously found to be the key to successful coordination.

Recently, multiple stakeholders reported that a more coordinated federal effort—possibly managed at the department level—could help to ensure a more adequate supply and distribution of the health care workforce, especially given changes in the delivery of care. For example, in examining federal GME funding, IOM and COGME each stated that the GME program lacks the oversight and infrastructure to track outcomes, reward performance, and respond to emerging workforce challenges.[36] IOM's recommendations for reforming GME include developing a strategic plan for oversight of GME funding, as well as taking steps to modernize GME payment methods based on performance to ensure program oversight and accountability. Both entities suggested that GME payments are neither sustainable in the long run nor the most effective method to developing the health care workforce to meet future projected health care needs. In each case, the organization recommended the creation of a new entity to provide oversight of national workforce efforts.[37] Moreover, Congress also recognized the need for greater coordinated attention to workforce planning when it authorized the creation of the National Health Care Workforce Commission. Although the Commission has not received an appropriation, it was authorized to provide advice to HHS and Congress about workforce supply and demand and to study various mechanisms to finance education and training. According to HHS officials, to the extent possible, the department has been able to complete work related to a number of the Commission's planned functions, but certain critical functions remain unaddressed. For example, the Commission would have been required to submit an annual report to Congress and the administration that would include, among other things, information on implications of current federal policies affecting the health care workforce and on workforce needs of underserved populations. Without a comprehensive and consistently coordinated approach, it will be difficult for HHS to ensure that workforce funding and other resources are aligned with future health needs and to provide effective oversight of this funding.

Some of HHS's Largest Health Care Workforce Programs Do Not Target Areas of Need, but HHS Has Made Some Improvements within Statutory Limitations

Some of HHS's largest health care workforce programs do not target areas of identified workforce needs. While HHS's ability to adjust existing programs to target areas of emerging needs is subject to certain statutory limitations, the department has taken some steps and proposed new authorities that would allow it to better align certain programs to areas of national need. However, the proposed authorities may not fully address the alignment of HHS's largest workforce programs with national needs.

HHS's Largest Health Care Workforce Programs Do Not Target Areas of Identified Need, Although Smaller Programs Do

Our review showed that although HHS's health care workforce programs support education and training for multiple professions, the biggest programs do not specifically target areas of workforce need. The two CMS Medicare GME programs, which accounted for 77 percent of HHS's fiscal year 2014 obligations for health care workforce development, support hospital-based training of the many different types of physician specialties. However, HHS cannot specifically target existing Medicare GME program funds to projected workforce needs—such as primary care and rural areas— because the disbursement of these funds is governed by requirements unrelated to workforce shortages.[38] As a result, the majority of Medicare GME funding is disbursed based on historical patterns. Therefore the Medicare-supported residency slots, supported by this Medicare GME funding, are most highly concentrated in northeastern states.[39] However, the areas of emerging health workforce need identified by HRSA in its health care workforce projection reports include the supply of primary care physicians, as well as various physician and non-physician providers in rural communities as well as ambulatory settings across the country.[40] According to the Rand Corporation, between 1996 and 2011, the number of primary care residents has increased 8.4 percent, while there has been a 10.3 percent increase in other specialties and a 61.1 percent increase in subspecialty residents, such as cardiology.

In contrast, HHS's smaller health care workforce programs typically target emerging health care workforce needs. For example, HRSA's five largest health care workforce education and training programs, which accounted for about 4 percent of HHS's workforce obligations in fiscal year 2014, targeted the health professions identified as areas of need, such as primary care physicians and nurse professions, including registered nurses.

HHS Has Limited Authority to Target Health Care Workforce Programs to Areas of Need and Has Taken Some Steps to Do So

According to HHS officials, the department generally has limited authority to better target workforce programs to address projected health care workforce needs. Our review showed that funding for many of the largest HHS health care workforce programs—for example, CMS's Medicare GME program—are governed by statutory requirements unrelated to workforce needs. Specifically, the funding formulas for 5 of the 12 largest programs that we reviewed do not provide HHS with authority to realign funding for these specific programs to address projected workforce needs, while the remaining 7 programs provided the department with some flexibility to realign funding.[41] For all of these 7 programs, HRSA officials reported that the agency has been able to exercise some flexibility in reallocating resources within a program or between similar programs, subject to existing law.[42]

HHS officials stated that although they have no authority to realign funding for programs governed by formula, the department has utilized other authorities to better align resources with health care needs. According to these officials, the agency has used demonstration authorities to test new payment models for the Medicaid GME program.[43] HHS officials identified several demonstration projects approved by CMS for states and residency programs using their GME funds. For example, the State Innovation Model demonstration at the Center for Medicare and Medicaid Innovation is providing financial and technical support to states for the development and testing of state-led, multi-payer health care payment and service delivery models that are intended to improve health system performance, increase quality of care, and decrease costs for Medicare, Medicaid, and Children's Health Insurance Program beneficiaries–and for residents of participating states.[44] According to HHS, a number of states are using the opportunity of participating in the demonstration to reform GME and make investments in the physician training more accountable. Both Vermont and Connecticut have been awarded funding as "model testing states" based on their state innovation proposals. HHS indicated that these states proposed innovative GME mechanisms, outside of those traditionally supported by CMS, to help better meet their health workforce needs.

HHS officials also reported that the Center for Medicare and Medicaid Innovation conducted demonstrations to test new approaches to paying providers.[45] For example, in 2012, the center initiated the graduate nurse education demonstration to increase the number of graduate nursing students enrolled in advance practice registered nurse training programs.

The demonstration increased reimbursement for their clinical training by $200 million over 4 years.[46]

HHS's Proposed Authorities May Not Fully Address Alignment of Its Largest Workforce Programs with National Needs

HHS has proposed additional authorities intended to help address changing health care workforce needs, although they may not fully align the department's programs with national needs. In both fiscal years 2015 and 2016, the President's budget proposed to reduce a portion of Medicare's GME payments made to hospitals by 10 percent.[47] It also proposed investing in a new program to provide additional GME funding for primary care and rural communities. The 10-year, $5.3 billion "targeted support" grant to be run by HRSA would build upon the work of HRSA's Teaching Health Centers Graduate Medical Education Payment Program and would train 13,000 physicians in primary care or other high-need specialties in teaching hospitals and other community-based health care facilities, with a focus on ambulatory and preventive care. According to HHS officials, these proposals are intended to serve as a first step to improve the alignment of GME funding with health care needs. The fiscal year 2016 budget also proposed continuation of programs, authorized under PPACA and Health Care and Education Reconciliation Act of 2010 (HCERA), to provide primary care providers with higher Medicare and Medicaid payments as a way to incentivize health care providers to offer primary care services to Medicare and Medicaid beneficiaries.[48] HHS officials indicated that the implementation of these proposals would help officials recognize any successes and gaps, and, if necessary, they could then develop any additional proposals to supplement the programs.[49] However, while implementing these proposed programs would provide greater funding to some areas of need, HHS officials stated that they do not know the full extent to which these proposals are sufficient to address identified health care workforce needs. While HHS officials indicated that the department planned to determine their sufficiency and identify remaining gaps after these proposals were enacted, the department does not have a comprehensive plan from which to evaluate the impact of the new programs or make a complete assessment of any gaps.

External stakeholders—such as IOM, Medicare Payment Advisory Commission (MedPAC), and COGME—have identified various reforms to HHS's largest health care workforce programs to better target these programs to emerging areas of health care workforce need. HHS officials told us that some of the reforms proposed by these stakeholders were the basis for some of the department's past budget and legislative proposals. For example, IOM convened a panel of experts that recommended restructuring Medicare GME payments to help align the programs to the health needs of the nation.[50] In its 2014 report, IOM proposed, among other things, (a) developing a new center at CMS to administer GME program payment reform and manage demonstrations of new GME payment models and (b) the creation of a transformation fund within the GME programs to finance payment demonstrations. In a report released in 2014, COGME concurred with IOM that there is a need to reform GME payments and, among other things, recommended expanding the GME program's clinical training environment into the ambulatory and community setting.[51] While an advocate for teaching hospitals— Association of American Medical Colleges (AAMC)—has cautioned against reductions in GME funding, it has also proposed reforms to the GME program and Medicare payment policy to bolster primary care training and reduce geographic disparities.[52]

CONCLUSION

While HHS maintains that developing an adequate supply and distribution of the health care workforce is a priority for the department, it has removed explicit language about goals and objectives related to workforce issues from its current strategic plan, which is the primary planning mechanism to address this issue. HHS's lack of specific planning goals for the health workforce in its current strategic plan makes it challenging for the department to plan and to maintain accountability. Moreover, the department does not currently have a comprehensive set of performance measures and targets to assess whether its workforce efforts and the specific individual workforce programs managed by its agencies are collectively meeting the department's broader strategic goal of strengthening health care by improving access and quality.

Because the responsibilities for HHS's workforce efforts, programs, and resources are dispersed among many agencies, it is important that HHS have a department-wide approach regarding its strategies and the actions needed to ensure an adequate supply and distribution of the nation's workforce. For example, while HRSA manages the largest number of workforce programs and the development of workforce projections, the vast majority of workforce development funds are administered by CMS— for which workforce planning is not a key mission. It is also important for HHS to comprehensively assess the extent to which its many workforce programs, collectively, are adequate to address changing health care workforce needs. Multiple stakeholders have made recommendations to improve these programs. However, because the majority of workforce funds must be dispersed based on statutory requirements unrelated to projected workforce needs, HHS has limited options to retarget them. HHS has proposed additional authorities in the past, but these have not been enacted, and HHS officials acknowledge that these additional authorities may not be sufficient to fully address the existing program limitations identified by stakeholders. Without a comprehensive and coordinated approach to program planning, HHS cannot fully identify the gaps between existing programs and national needs, identify actions needed to address these gaps, or determine whether additional legislative proposals are needed to ensure that its programs fully meet workforce needs.

RECOMMENDATION FOR EXECUTIVE ACTION

To ensure that HHS workforce efforts meet national needs, we recommend that the Secretary of Health and Human Services develop a comprehensive and coordinated planning approach to guide HHS's health care workforce development programs—including education, training, and payment programs—that

- includes performance measures to more clearly determine the extent to which these programs are meeting the department's strategic goal of strengthening health care;
- identifies and communicates to stakeholders any gaps between existing programs and future health care workforce needs identified in HRSA's workforce projection reports;
- identifies actions needed to address identified gaps; and
- identifies and communicates to Congress the legislative authority, if any, the Department needs to implement the identified actions.

AGENCY COMMENTS AND OUR EVALUATION

We provided a draft copy of this report to HHS for its review. In commenting on this draft, HHS concurred with our recommendation that it is important that the department have a comprehensive and coordinated approach to guide its health care workforce development programs. HHS identified areas where comprehensive and coordinated planning efforts are already underway and where additional efforts are needed.

HHS identified several health care workforce planning efforts related to the elements of our recommendation, many of which we described in the draft report. For example, HHS noted that it coordinates workforce planning efforts through the HHS department-level and agency-specific budget, legislative development, health policy research and innovation work, performance management, and strategic planning. HHS also indicated that the National Health Care Workforce Commission, created under PPACA, has the potential to enhance HHS's ability to implement a more comprehensive and coordinated planning approach, but that the commission has not received federal appropriations. In the absence of appropriations for this commission, HHS stated that it has undertaken some of the commission's health care workforce planning and coordination activities, to the extent possible. In response to our recommendation, HHS indicated that it could convene an interagency group to assess (a) existing workforce programs, (b) performance measurement, (c) budgetary and other proposals, (d) gaps in workforce programs, and (e) potential requests to the Congress for modified or expanded legislative authority. We agree that a regular and ongoing initiative focused on the coordination of health care workforce programs could provide an important first step toward ensuring a more comprehensive and coordinated planning approach.

HHS also reiterated that its health care workforce programs contribute to its broad goals of access and quality from its strategic plan, as was described in our draft report. However, it indicated that, in response to our recommendation, the department plans to add two new workforce-specific strategies to its strategic plan when it next updates the plan.

HHS also provided technical comments, which we incorporated as appropriate.

Kathleen M. King
Director, Health Care

APPENDIX I: PERFORMANCE MEASURES FOR SELECTED HHS HEALTH CARE WORKFORCE PROGRAMS, 2014

Program	Targeted health professional	# of performance measures	Meets/exceeds/ has not met performance targets
Centers for Medicare and Medicaid Services			
Medicare Indirect Medical Education Payments	Physicians, dentists, and podiatrists	None	Not applicable
Medicare Direct Graduate Medical Education (GME) Payments	Physicians, dentists, and podiatrists	None	Not applicable
Medicaid Payment for GME	Physicians, dentists, and podiatrists	None	Not applicable
Medicare Payments for Nursing and Allied Health Education	Nurse and allied professionals	None	Not applicable
Health Resources and Services Administration			
Children's Hospital GME	Primary care physicians and pediatric specialists	3 performance measures	Exceeds Meets Meets
National Health Service Corps (NHSC) Loan Repayment Program	Primary care physicians, advanced practice registered nurses, and others	4 performance measures	Exceeds Exceeds Exceeds Exceeds
NHSC Scholarship Program	Primary care physicians, advanced practice registered nurses, and others	Same as NHSC above	Same as NHSC above

Program	Targeted health professional	# of performance measures	Meets/exceeds/ has not met performance targets
Advanced Nursing Education	Advanced practice registered nurses	6 performance measures	Exceeds Exceeds Exceeds Exceeds Exceeds Exceeds
NURSE Corps Loan Repayment Program	Nurses	4 performance measures	Exceeds Not met Exceeds Exceeds
Scholarships for Disadvantaged Students	Multiple health professionals	3 performance measures	Exceeds Exceeds Not Met
Nurse Education Practice, Quality and Retention Grants[a]	Nurses	5 performance measures	Not met Not available Not available Not met Not met
Administration for Children and Families			
Health Profession Opportunity Grants	Multiple health professionals	None	Not applicable

Source: GAO analysis of HHS data. | GAO-16-17

Note:

[a] HHS indicated that this program has two new measures and targets that will be included in its fiscal year 2017 budget.

Appendix II: Goals, Objectives, Strategies, and Metrics from the HHS 2014-2018 Strategic Plan That Are Related to Health Care Workforce Development

Goal	Related Objectives	Related Strategies	Related Metrics
Goal One: Strengthen Health Care (1 of 4 Goals in the plan)	Objective E: Ensure access to quality, culturally competent care, including long-term services and support, for vulnerable populations (1 of 6 Objectives in Goal 1)	• Monitor access to and quality of care across population groups, and work with federal, state, local, tribal, urban Indian, and nongovernmental actors to address observed disparities and to encourage and facilitate consultation and collaboration among them.	•Field strength of the National Health Service Corps through scholarship and loan repayment agreements.[a] •Percentage of individuals supported by Bureau of Health Workforce

Appendix II. (Continued)

Goal	Related Objectives	Related Strategies	Related Metrics
		• Evaluate the impact of the Affordable Care Act provisions on access to and quality of care for vulnerable populations, as well as on disparities in access and quality. • Promote access to primary oral health care services and oral disease preventive services in settings including federally funded health centers, school-based health centers, and Indian Health Services-funded programs that have comprehensive primary oral health care services, and state and community-based programs that improve oral health, especially for children, pregnant women, older adults, and people with disabilities. • Help eliminate disparities in health care by educating and training physicians, nurses, and allied health professionals on disparities and cultural competency, while increasing workforce diversity in medical and allied health care professions. • Improve access to comprehensive primary and preventive medical services to historically underserved areas and support federally funded health centers, the range of services offered by these centers, and increased	Programs who completed a primary care training program and are currently employed in underserved areas.[b] (2 of 13 Metrics in Objective E)

Goal	Related Objectives	Related Strategies	Related Metrics
		coordination with partners including the Aging Services Network. (5 of 18 Strategies in Objective E)	
	Objective F: Improve health care and population health through meaningful use of health information technology (1 of 6 Objectives in Goal 1)	• Expand the adoption of telemedicine technologies, including more remote patient monitoring, electronic intensive care units, home health, and telemedicine networks, to increase access to health care services for people living in tribal, rural, and other underserved communities, and other vulnerable and hard-to-reach populations. (1 of 18 Strategies in Objective F)	None
Goal Four: Ensure Efficiency, Transparency, Accountability, and Effectiveness of HHS Programs (1 of 4 Goals in the plan)	Objective C: Invest in the HHS workforce to help meet America's health and human services needs (1 of 4 Objectives in Goal 4)	• Promote the Commissioned Corps as a health resource to provide public health services in hard-to-fill assignments as well as to respond to public health emergencies. (1 of 13 Strategies in Objective C)	None

Source: GAO analysis of HHS's strategic plan. | GAO-16-17

Notes:

[a]According to HHS officials, four programs are included in this metric: National Health Service Corps (NHSC) Loan Repayment Program, NHSC Scholarship Program, NHSC Students to Service Loan Repayment Program, and the State Loan Repayment Program.

[b]According to HHS officials, 14 programs are included in this metric: Academic Administrative Units in Primary Care; Advanced Education Nurse Traineeship; Graduate Psychology Education; Integrative Medicine Program; Nurse Anesthetist Traineeship; Physician Assistant Training in Primary Care; Pre-doctoral Training in General, Pediatric, and Public Health Dentistry and Dental Hygiene; Post-doctoral Training in General, Pediatric, and Public Health Dentistry; Preventive Medicine Residencies; Residency Training in Primary Care; Scholarships for Disadvantaged Students; State Oral Health Workforce; Teaching Health Centers; and Physician Faculty Development in Primary Care.

Appendix III: Goals and Strategies from HHS Agency Strategic Plans That Are Related to Health Care Workforce Development

Agency	Year	Goal	Related Strategies	Related Metrics
Administration for Children and Families	2015	Goal One: Promote Economic, Health, and Social Well-Being for Individuals, Families, and Communities	We will promote efforts to increase family economic security and stability by supporting our state, tribal, and community grantee partners in designing and implementing programs that focus simultaneously on parental employment and child and family well-being, including drawing from promising models in health and career pathways demonstrations.	None
Centers for Medicare and Medicaid Services	2013	None	None	None
Health Resources and Services Administration	2016	Goal Two: Strengthen the Health Workforce	• Support curriculum development and the training of health professionals to ensure the learning, enhancement, and updating of essential knowledge and skills. • Support training and other activities that enhance the health workforce's competency in providing culturally and linguistically appropriate care. • Expand the number and type of training and technical assistance opportunities that educate students and providers to work in inter professional teams and participate in practice transformations.	• Field strength of the National Health Service Corps through scholarship and loan repayment agreements. • Percentage of individuals supported by the Bureau of Health Workforce who completed a primary care training program and are currently employed in underserved areas.

Agency	Year	Goal	Related Strategies	Related Metrics
			• Support technical assistance, training, and other opportunities to help safety-net providers expand, coordinate, and effectively use health information technology to support service delivery and quality improvement. • Provide information and technical assistance to ensure that HRSA-supported safety-net providers know and use current treatment guidelines, appropriate promising practices, and evidence-based models of care. • Facilitate and support the recruitment, placement, and retention of primary care and other providers in underserved communities in order to address shortages and improve the distribution of the health workforce. • Support outreach and other activities to increase the recruitment, training, placement, and retention of under-represented groups in the health workforce.	• Percentage of trainees in Bureau of Health Workforce-supported health professions training programs who receive training in medically underserved communities. • Percentage of trainees in Bureau of Health Workforce programs who are underrepresented minorities and/or from disadvantaged backgrounds.
Health Resources and Services Administration (cont.)			• Support pre-entry academic advising, mentoring, and enrichment activities for underrepresented groups in order to promote successful health professions training and career development. • Promote training opportunities within community-based settings for health professions students and residents by enhancing partnerships with organizations serving the underserved.	

Appendix III. (Continued)

Agency	Year	Goal	Related Strategies	Related Metrics
			• Develop and employ approaches to monitoring, forecasting, and meeting long-term health workforce needs. • Provide policy makers, researchers, and the public with information on health workforce trends, supply, demand, and policy issues.	
Indian Health Service (IHS)	2006a	Not applicable[a]	• Not applicable	Not applicable[a]
Substance Abuse and Mental Health Services Administration[b]	2015	Goal Six: Workforce Development	• Develop and disseminate workforce training and education tools and core competencies to address behavioral health issues. •Develop and support deployment of peer providers in all public health and health care delivery settings. •Develop consistent data collection methods to identify and track behavioral health care workforce needs.	• Increase the number of behavioral health providers (professional, paraprofessional, and peers) addressing children, adolescents, and transitional-age youth. •Increase the number of individuals trained as behavioral health peer providers.

Source: GAO analysis of strategic plans for HHS agencies. | GAO-16-17

Notes:

[a]IHS officials said that IHS last updated its strategic plan in 2006, and it is now out of date. Officials stated that IHS programs are aligned with the HHS strategic plan through Strategic Goal One, Objective E. Moreover, HHS officials told us that in updating IHS's strategic plan to its current version, they received input from various entities, including IHS.

[b]HHS officials stated that the department has an additional strategy of influencing and supporting funding for the behavioral health workforce and an additional metric of increasing the percentage of reimbursement rates and potential pay incentives associated with the development of a prospective payment system.

End Notes

[1] For the purpose of this report, the "health care workforce" includes those professionals who provide direct health care, including, but not limited to, audiologists, chiropractors, dentists, medical assistants, nurses, occupational therapists, optometrists, pharmacists, physical therapists, physicians, physician assistants, podiatrists, psychologists, social workers, and counselors.

[2] See GAO, *Health Care Workforce: Federal Investments in Training and the Availability of Data for Workforce Projections,* GAO-14-510T (Washington, D.C.: Apr. 9, 2014); and U.S. Department of Health and Human Services, *A 21st Century Health Care Workforce for the Nation* (Washington, D.C.: February 2014).

[3] According to officials of the Department of Health and Human Services (HHS), the HHS models that predict workforce shortages generally assume that health care continues to be provided in the manner that it is currently provided. However, changes in the way that health care services are delivered in the future might alter the demand for health care services and professionals, and the impact of new and existing technology is difficult to predict. See, for example, A. Grover and L. M. Niecko-Najjum, "Building a Health Care Workforce for the Future: More Physicians, Professional Reforms, and Technological Advances," *Health Affairs*, vol. 32, no.11 (2013):1922-1927; and T. S. Bodenheimer and M. Smith, "Primary Care: Proposed Solutions to the Physician Shortage without Training More Physicians," *Health Affairs*, vol. 32, no. 11 (2013): 1881-1886.

[4] T. Bodenheimer and A. Fernandez, "High and Rising Health Care Costs. Part 4: Can Costs be Controlled While Preserving Quality," *Annals of Internal Medicine*, vol. 143, no. 1 (2005); J. P. Weiner, S. Yeh, and D. Blumenthal, "The Impact of Health Information Technology and e-Health on the Future Demand For Physician Services," *Health Affairs*, vol. 32, no.11 (2013): 1998-2004; and D. I. Auerbach, P. G. Chen, M. W. Friedberg, R. O. Reid, C. Lau, and A. Mehrotra, "Nurse-Managed Health Centers and Patient-Centered Medical Homes Could Mitigate Expected Primary Care Physician Shortage," *Health Affairs*, vol. 32, no. 11 (2013): 1933–1941.

[5] In addition to HHS, other federal agencies—such as the Departments of Defense and Veterans Affairs—also support health care workforce development programs. States have also played a role in health care workforce development. Several states have health care workforce initiatives designed to fill certain gaps in the health care workforce.

For this report, we focused on HHS education, training, and payment programs that supported postsecondary training or education for direct health care professionals by directly providing or funding one or more of the following services—instruction or formal training opportunities; on-the-job clinical training for postgraduate health professionals; financial assistance for health professional students or professionals; or patient care-related continuing education for direct care health professionals if such training was the main program service provided. We excluded workforce programs that assist in the education and training of the public health workforce, individuals pursuing biomedical research careers, or programs that are strictly for information dissemination.

[6] In this report we refer to HHS component agencies as "HHS agency" or "agency".

[7] Pub. L. No. 111-148, 124 Stat. 119, (2010) as amended by the Health Care and Education Reconciliation Act of 2010, (HCERA), Pub. L. No. 111-152, 124 Stat. 1029. Throughout this report, references to PPACA include amendments made by HCERA.

[8] See GAO, *Health Care Workforce: HRSA Action Needed to Publish Timely National Supply and Demand Projections*, GAO-13-806 (Washington, D.C.: Sept. 30, 2013). In this report,

we recommended that the department expedite and publish national projections for the primary care workforce and develop tools to monitor report review to ensure timeline goals for publication of the projection reports are met. HHS has implemented these recommendations.

[9] These agencies are the Administration for Children and Families (ACF), CMS, HRSA, the Indian Health Service (IHS), and the Substance Abuse and Mental Health Services Administration (SAMHSA).

[10] Pub. L. No. 111-352, 124 Stat. 3866 (2011). GPRAMA amended the Government Performance and Results Act of 1993 (GPRA), the statutory framework for performance management in the federal government. Pub. L. No. 103-62, 107 Stat. 285 (1993). GPRAMA established new requirements aimed at a more crosscutting and integrated approach to focusing on results and improving government performance.

[11] See, for example, GAO, *Executive Guide: Effectively Implementing the Government Performance and Results Act*, GAO/GGD-96-118 (Washington, D.C.: June 1996).

[12] Starting with the list of 69 programs that we identified in our 2013 report (GAO-13-806), in February 2015 we asked each HHS agency to update its list of programs. This process resulted in a list of 72 programs that were funded in fiscal year 2014.

[13] The results of our review of these 12 programs are not generalizable to all of HHS's health care workforce programs.

[14] These consist of 10 reports by HRSA's National Center for Health Workforce Analysis, Washington, D.C.: *Projecting the Supply and Demand for Primary Care Practitioners Through 2020* (November 2013); *Projecting the Supply of Non-Primary Care Specialty and Subspecialty Clinicians: 2010-2025* (July 2014); *National- and State-Level Projections of Dentists and Dental Hygienists in the U.S., 2012-2025* (February 2015); *Health Workforce Projections: Vision Occupations* (December 2014); *Health Workforce Projections: Occupational Therapy and Physical Therapy* (December 2014); *Health Workforce Projections: Pharmacists* (December 2014); *The Future of the Nursing Workforce: National- and State-Level Projections, 2012-2025* (December 2014); *Health Workforce Projections: Respiratory Therapists* (April 2015); *Health Workforce Projections: Psychologists* (April 2015); and *Health Workforce Projections: Chiropractors and Podiatrists* (April 2015).

[15] The 2010-2015 HHS strategic plan listed "performance measures" that were used to track performance, while the 2014-2018 HHS strategic plan used "performance goals" for the same purpose. For this engagement we use the term performance measures. See http://www.hhs.gov/about/strategic-plan/message/index.html.

[16] U.S. Department of Health and Human Services, *Fiscal Year 2016 Annual Performance Plan and Report* (Washington, D.C.: February 2015).

[17] The Office of the Surgeon General and the Office of Population Affairs also fund health care workforce programs, obligating less than $5 million combined in fiscal year 2014.

[18] See http://bhpr.hrsa.gov/healthworkforce/supplydemand/usworkforce/projections/index.html.

[19] In 2013 and 2014, we reported that publication of these reports had been delayed. See GAO-13-806 and GAO-14-510T. As of April 2015, HRSA had published reports on primary care, clinical specialty professions, dentists, vision occupations, occupational and physical therapists, pharmacists, nurses, respiratory therapists, psychologists, chiropractors, and podiatrists. Workforce projections for behavioral health professionals were due to be released in the fall of 2015.

[20] Workforce development efforts involving HHS's employees are included in the 2014- 2018 HHS Strategic Plan within a separate goal—ensuring efficiency, transparency, accountability, and effectiveness of HHS programs. See app. II for more details.

[21] IHS officials said that IHS last updated its strategic plan in 2006, and it is now out of date. Officials stated that IHS programs are aligned with the HHS 2014-2018 strategic plan through Strategic Goal One, Objective E. Moreover, HHS officials told us that in updating the HHS strategic plan to its current version, they received input from various entities, including IHS.

[22] GAO, *Executive Guide: Effectively Implementing the Government Performance and Results Act*, GAO/GGD-96-118 (Washington, D.C.: June 1996). We identified similar coordination challenges with other federal crosscutting programs. See, for example, GAO, *Mental Health: HHS Leadership Needed to Coordinate Federal Efforts Related to Serious Mental Illness*, GAO-15-113 (Washington, D.C.: Dec. 18, 2014).

[23] See U.S. Department of Health and Human Services, *Foster a 21st Century Health Workforce*, accessed 11/12/2014, www.hhs.gov/strategic-plan/health-workforce.html. Document no longer available online.

[24] U.S. Department of Health and Human Services, *A 21st Century Health Care Workforce for the Nation* (Washington, D.C.: February 2014), accessed October 1, 2014, http://aspe.hhs.gov/health/reports/2014/HealthCare_Workforce/rpt_healthcareworkforce.pdf.

[25] The department also reports program specific performance measures through a variety of publications such as the annual budget justification and the Summary of Performance and Financial Information.

[26] These two measures are the 1) field strength of the National Health Service Corps through scholarship and loan repayment agreements and 2) percentage of individuals supported by Bureau of Health Workforce programs that completed a primary care training program and are currently employed in underserved areas.

[27] According to HHS officials, the agency's annual performance plan and report must capture the breadth of the programs implemented by HHS in a format that is consumable by the public.

[28] According to HHS, the department's target for the first measure is that 100 percent of Americans have access to a usual source of care.

[29] According to HHS officials, those programs without performance measures use a cost reporting system as the mechanism to ensure oversight and accountability. For example, the GME programs are funded activities that are not managed through a grant; therefore, they do not have a "performance management" system. However, HHS officials indicated that CMS uses its cost reports to track data on where the GME funding goes.

[30] Medicare is a federally financed program that provides health insurance coverage to people age 65 and older, certain individuals with disabilities, and those with end-stage renal disease.

[31] GAO, *Executive Guide: Effectively Implementing the Government Performance and Results Act*, GAO/GGD-96-118 (Washington, D.C.: June 1996).

[32] For example, according to agency officials, HRSA is the primary federal agency for improving access to health care and manages 49 of the 72 workforce training and education programs; SAMHSA has several programs related to training mental health and substance use disorder providers; ACF assists in the placement of low-income individuals into the health care field; CMS oversees payments to Medicare providers and therefore handles GME payments; and IHS encourages the placement of physicians into Indian health care facilities.

[33] For example, HRSA and SAMHSA supported a projection report for the behavioral health workforce that is scheduled to be released in the fall of 2015.

[34] GAO, *Managing for Results: Implementation Approaches Used to Enhance Collaboration in Interagency Groups*, GAO-14-220 (Washington, D.C.: Feb. 14, 2014).

[35] GAO, *Mental Health: HHS Leadership Needed to Coordinate Federal Efforts Related to Serious Mental Illness*, GAO-15-113 (Washington, D.C.: Dec. 18, 2014).

[36] Institute of Medicine, *Graduate Medical Education That Meets the Nation's Health Needs* (Washington, D.C.: 2014); and Council on Graduate Medical Education, *Twenty-Second Report: The Role of Graduate Medical Education in the New Health Paradigm* (Washington, D.C.: November 2014).

[37] Among other things, IOM recommended steps to modernize GME payment methods based on performance, to ensure program oversight and accountability, and to incentivize innovation in the content and financing of GME.

[38] 42 U.S.C. §§ 1395ww(d)(5)(B), 1395ww(h)(2).

[39] According to a 2014 IOM report, Medicare supported residency positions are essentially frozen in place without regard for future changes in local or regional health care workforce priorities or the geography or demography of the U.S. population. IOM also reported that the location of a doctor's medical school is predictive of his practice location, and that the longer a doctor trains in a particular area, the more likely the doctor will practice there.

[40] Provider shortages are also anticipated in the fields of dentistry, cardiology, behavioral health, and general surgery.

[41] The five formula-based payment programs are Medicare Indirect Medical Education Payments, Medicare Direct Graduate Medical Education, Medicaid Payments for GME, Medicare Payments for Nursing and Allied Health Education, and Children's Hospital GME. HHS officials stated that in the absence of authority to direct GME funds to national needs, HHS is focused on improving access to care for the nation, and in particular the safety net, through its other workforce programs.

[42] For example, in fiscal year 2015, HRSA combined four geriatric programs into one program—the Geriatric Workforce Enhancement Program—to attempt to improve health outcomes for older adults by integrating geriatrics with primary care. In July 2015, $35.7 million was awarded to the program.

[43] Medicaid is a joint federal-state program that finances health care coverage for certain low-income individuals.

[44] Section 3021 of PPACA established the Center for Medicare and Medicaid Innovation and authorized the selection of models to test using the funds appropriated to it in that section. Pub. L. No. 111-148, §§ 3021, 10306, 124 Stat. 119, 389, 939 (codified at 42 U.S.C. § 1315a). See also GAO, *CMS Innovation Center: Early Implementation Efforts Suggest Need for Additional Actions to Help Ensure Coordination with Other CMS Offices*, GAO-13-12 (Washington, D.C.: Nov. 15, 2012).

[45] See GAO, *CMS Innovation Center: Early Implementation Efforts Suggest Need for Additional Actions to Help Ensure Coordination with Other CMS Offices*, GAO-13-12 (Washington, D.C.: Nov. 15, 2012).

[46] See http://innovation.cms.gov/initiatives/gne/ for more details.

[47] In these budgets, the President proposed reducing indirect GME payments made to hospitals. Moreover, the President also proposed setting standards for teaching hospitals to encourage training of primary care residents and emphasize skills that promote high-quality and high-value health care. According to HHS officials, the legislative authorities sought in these budgets have, to date, not been enacted by Congress. The President made this same proposal in fiscal year 2014 and past budgets have also proposed reforms to GME funding.

[48] PPACA provides for a 10 percent bonus Medicare payment for certain primary care services furnished by eligible primary care providers through 2015. HCERA provides that eligible primary care providers furnishing certain Medicaid primary care services be paid at the Medicare rate through 2014. Pub. L. No. 111-148, § 5501(a), 124 Stat. 119, 652 (2010); Pub. L. No. 111-152, § 1202, 124 Stat. 1029, 1052 (2010). Specifically, the budget proposed $6.3 billion to extend the Medicaid primary care payment increase enacted in PPACA and HCERA through 2016 and to include additional providers. The Medicare Payment Advisory Commission (MedPAC)—an advisory body to Congress on Medicare policy—also endorsed continuation of higher Medicare payments to primary care providers in its 2015 report to Congress to increase access to primary care.

[49] HHS officials we interviewed told us that the department is developing additional proposals for fiscal year 2017 to reform workforce programs. These reform proposals are under discussion within HHS and its agencies and, once completed, may be included in the President's fiscal year 2017 budget.

[50] Institute of Medicine, *Graduate Medical Education That Meets the Nation's Health Needs* (Washington, D.C.: 2014). IOM found that the current GME structure and financing lacks the oversight and infrastructure to track outcomes, reward performance, and respond nimbly to emerging workforce challenges.

[51] Council on Graduate Medical Education, *Twenty-Second Report: The Role of Graduate Medical Education in the New Health Care Paradigm* (November 2014).

[52] For example, in 2012, AAMC recommended that additional GME training positions be created and that half of these new positions be targeted to primary care and generalist disciplines. AAMC also recommended that payment policy be used to affect the geographic distribution of physicians and make certain clinical specialties more attractive to doctors.

In: U.S. Health Care Workforce
Editor: Sheldon T. Barrett
ISBN: 978-1-63485-730-7

Chapter 14

A 21ST CENTURY HEALTH CARE WORKFORCE FOR THE NATION*

U.S. Department of Health and Human Services

I. OVERVIEW

The 2015 President's Budget proposes major new investments to build the health care workforce and improve the delivery of health care services, particularly primary care services, across the nation.

Key components of this Presidential initiative are:

- *Modernizing Graduate Medical Education*: Create an updated approach to residency training by targeting $5.23 billion in mandatory funds to an innovative competitive grant program to create new residency slots with a focus on community-based ambulatory care. This program will be administered by the Health Resources and Services Administration (HRSA). It is expected to produce 13,000 physicians over the next ten years and advance key workforce goals, including the training of more physicians in primary care and other high need specialties, aligning training with more efficient and effective care delivery models, and encouraging physicians to practice in underserved areas including rural areas.

---

* This is an edited, reformatted and augmented version of a report issued by the U.S. Department of Health and Human Services, February 2014.

- *National Health Service Corps (NHSC):* Expand the Corps to increase the availability of providers in those areas across the country most in need. Over the next 6 years, the Department will devote $3.95 billion in mandatory funds to the NHSC which will greatly expand the number of NHSC health care providers in underserved areas from fewer than 8,900 to an annual field strength of 15,000 for each year from 2015 through 2020.
- *Extend Enhanced Medicaid Primary Care Payments:* Extend the Affordable Care Act's (ACA's) enhanced Medicaid primary care payments through Calendar Year (CY) 2015 to better target primary care and expand eligibility to mid-level providers practicing independently, at an estimated cost of $5.44 billion. The ACA requires Medicaid reimbursement for primary care services furnished by eligible physicians to be increased to the Medicare rates for CYs 2013 and 2014.

This initiative builds on the Administration's continuing efforts using a variety of policy tools across agencies within the Department of Health and Human Services to help assure that the nation's health care workforce can meet the challenges of 21st century health care delivery.

Investments from the American Recovery and Reinvestment Act of 2009 (ARRA) and the ACA have helped lay the ground work for this workforce initiative, and they, in turn, are built upon both long-standing and evolving workforce development efforts across the Department, particularly in the Centers for Medicare and Medicaid Services (CMS) and HRSA.

Key Principles

Guiding this endeavor are five principles for workforce reform:

1) moving toward a value-based system,
2) using workforce levers to improve access to primary care,
3) making full use of every member of the health care team,
4) aligning the workforce to population needs, and
5) transforming health care delivery through workforce innovation

II. INTRODUCTION

The President's budget proposals seek to increase the number of providers trained and better match the supply and distribution of well-trained health care personnel to meet the needs of the nation's evolving health care delivery system. Much of the Department's focus has been on expanding access to primary care services.

A number of factors influence the contemporary health care workforce's ability to meet emerging demands. Among these factors are population growth, the aging of the population, the growing burden of chronic diseases across all age groups, the adoption of new technologies in medical practice, the anticipated retirement of baby boom health care practitioners, and the expansion of insurance coverage to millions of Americans through the ACA. These factors play out against an existing workforce that is maldistributed geographically and across specialties and is sometimes in short supply. The Department proposes to meet these challenges with a multi-pronged policy agenda that promotes the effective delivery of high quality care while constraining costs.

The Department has long promoted a health care workforce that provides high quality, cost- effective, culturally competent care; possesses the skills and tools necessary for delivering that care; and sees innovative delivery system reform as a means to improve care delivery for patients. This report highlights the Department's 2015 workforce budget proposals as well as certain other efforts to make full use of each member of the health care team, better align the health workforce to population needs, promote skills and tools for delivering high quality care, and through existing policy levers use the health workforce to transform health care delivery. It is not intended to be an exhaustive list of the workforce accomplishments of ARRA and the ACA, which have been summarized in other documents[1].

III. BACKGROUND ON THE HEALTH CARE WORKFORCE

The American health care workforce includes more than 14 million people[2], and accounts for about 10 percent of the national workforce. This total includes those employed within the health sector, in hospitals, clinics, practitioners' offices and nursing homes, as well as those employed in other sites such as insurance companies, worksites, schools, and government at all levels. The workforce job classifications encompass a rich mix of occupation types and professional qualifications. The largest numbers by category are found in registered nurses (2.8 million), nursing, psychiatric and home health aides (2.3 million), personal care aides (1 million), physicians (861,000), medical assistants and other health care support personnel (845,000) and licensed practical and licensed vocational nurses (690,000)[3].

This paper focuses on clinical care health professionals, and in particular those providing or supporting primary care, including the nearly 300,000 physicians, nurse practitioners, and physician assistants and their support staff who collectively provide the integrated, accessible, first contact health care that addresses a majority of most individuals' health care needs. It does not specifically address the long term care work force and direct care workers although some of this paper's themes are applicable to this group as well.

A Word about Workforce Data

The Affordable Care Act strengthened health care workforce data collection and analysis activities by authorizing the National Center for Health Workforce Analysis. Located in the Health Resources and Services Administration (HRSA), the Center is charged with building the body of knowledge about the nation's health care workforce through data development and projections of supply and demand and serving as a focal point for health workforce data upon which policy can be built as the health care system evolves to meet emerging demands. This paper draws on reports from the Center (available here: http://bhpr.hrsa.gov/health workforce/)

In addition to the work of the National Center, enhancements to the National Center for Health Statistics' National Ambulatory Medical Care Survey over the past several years shed valuable light on the current practice of ambulatory medicine on topics such as the use of electronic health records by office-based physicians.

IV. Policy Levers

The Department has a range of policy levers to help address the composition of the health care workforce, its training and education, geographic distribution, and the ability to experiment with new delivery system and payment models. However, some workforce functions are inherently non-federal. States oversee the licensing and regulation of health professions, defining the scope of practice of individual professions, and setting minimum standards for entry and licensure, often drawing on input from professional societies. States, the private sector, and academic institutions invest in workforce education and have roles in determining how many people are trained in what disciplines. The work of independent entities such as the Accreditation Council on Graduate Medical Education which accredits post-medical school training programs and the American Board of Medical Specialties which assists specialty societies in the development and implementation of standards for medical specialty certification provides valuable input into workforce policy. Federal influence over workforce policy includes:

- Medicare and Medicaid payment policy
- Graduate Medical Education and other workforce training programs
- Loan and scholarship programs
- Promotion of quality and efficiency through delivery system reform

A. Medicare and Medicaid Payment Policy

Commentators have said that the way Medicare and many other health care purchasers pay for physician services undervalues primary care and other medical care that is not procedure-focused. That can lead to medical students choosing specialty care over primary care in part because of better lifetime earnings. In the past Medicare has offered incentive add-ons to its normal payments to influence practitioner behavior. One longstanding example is the Health Professional Shortage Area (HPSA) incentive payment whereby physicians who furnish Medicare-covered services within a geographic HPSA are paid a 10 percent bonus above what they would have otherwise been paid. The ACA builds on this model by -- for the years 2011 through 2015 -- providing a 10 percent incentive payment, the Primary Care Incentive Payment (PCIP), on top of the fee schedule payment for select primary care services. To qualify for the bonus, physicians must be self-designated in a primary care specialty (general internal medicine, family practice, pediatrics, and geriatrics) and a substantial portion—at least 60 percent—of their Medicare billings must be for designated primary care services[4]. Of particular note, unlike the HPSA incentive payment, this payment is also extended to nurse practitioners and physician assistants.

The Department has announced its intention to begin paying, in January 2015, for chronic care management services for beneficiaries with complex needs. These services must be provided by practices meeting standards necessary to furnish high quality, comprehensive, and safe chronic care management services. It is expected that this will encourage coordination across provider types and locations and encourage non-face-toface patient contact through, for example, telephone or internet encounters. The ACA also contained a provision that required Medicaid to reimburse primary care services provided by eligible physicians at no less than Medicare rates during calendar years 2013 and 2014. While Medicaid physician payment on average was approximately 65 percent that of Medicare, primary care payment lagged further at only 59 percent of Medicare rates[5]. This provision in the President's budget will help expand access for Medicaid patients as many States expand their Medicaid programs. Its longer duration will help influence physician behavior and extending the provision to independently practicing nurse practitioners and physician assistants will expand the number of eligible providers.

> Enhanced Medicaid Primary Care Payments: The President's 2015 budget request broadens eligibility for this increased payment to mid-level providers, better targets primary care, and extends the program for an additional year.

Medicare is improving the way it pays for physician services. The Center for Medicare and Medicaid Innovation (Innovation Center) is exploring new payment models and service delivery models, including some models that are testing movement away from payment based solely on the number of procedures or services delivered to patients and towards models that reward high quality, patient-centered care. Established through the ACA, with $10 billion in funding for FYs 2011-2019, the Innovation Center is charged with testing innovative payment and service delivery models designed to maintain or improve the quality of care furnished to Medicare, Medicaid, and Children's Health Insurance Program beneficiaries and reduce program expenditures. The ACA permits expansion, including implementation on a nationwide basis of the duration and scope of the model tested by the Innovation Center. Models may be expanded if the expansion is expected to reduce spending without reducing the quality of care or improve the quality of care without increasing spending. The Chief Actuary of the CMS must certify that contemplated expansions not increase net spending. Currently 18 major service delivery and payment models are being tested. Innovation Center demonstrations are discussed in more detail later in this paper.

B. Graduate Medical Education and Other Workforce Training Programs

The Medicare program supports graduate medical education (GME) through a system of two payments to teaching hospitals. Direct Medical Education (DME) payments take the form of Medicare paying its share of a hospital's per resident costs from a base year and trended forward. The number of residents supported in this way by Medicare has been capped since 1997. Teaching hospitals also receive Indirect Medical Education (IME) payments through an adjustment to the diagnosis-related group payment for each Medicare covered in-patient stay to take into account the higher costs of teaching hospitals. Together these two types of payments are projected to total $11.2 billion in 2014, approximately $3.3 billion for DME and $7.9 billion for IME. (Most states also make GME payments through their Medicaid programs. As of 2012, 42 states and the District of Columbia made GME payments through their Medicaid programs, with an estimated total Medicaid spending of $3.87 billion[6].) Observers have noted that GME slots and spending are not evenly distributed, with large differences across the states in the number of residents supported, and per capita GME spending, with an imbalance not attuned to those states now growing in population[7]. The location of the residency is a strong predictor of where a physician ultimately practices[8]. The ACA required the redistribution of unused GME slots, with 70 percent of redistributed slots allocated to those states whose resident-to-population ratios were in the lowest quartile.

In assessing graduate medical education in a 2010 report[9], the Medicare Payment Advisory Commission (MedPAC) found that these current funding mechanisms are not optimally aligned to produce the medical workforce needed in the future, highlighting increased specialization and limited racial and socioeconomic diversity among residents. MedPAC also noted that IME payments were significantly in excess of hospital costs associated with medical education and suggested pairing a reduction in funding for IME with increased support for high quality primary care training. As in the past two years and again this year, the President's budget is proposing reducing by 10 percent IME payments and better aligning these payments with Department priorities. This proposal would give the Secretary authority to set standards for teaching hospitals receiving GME payments to encourage the training of primary care residents and an emphasis on skills that promote high-quality and high-value health care delivery.

A new HRSA grant program, Targeted Support for Graduate Medical Education, proposed in the 2015 budget request, builds on the ACA GME provisions and is an important first step in better shaping graduate medical education to align with national needs. This grant program will be funded through transfers from the Medicare Hospital Insurance (HI) Trust Fund and is a way of encouraging innovation in training models and greater accountability in the use of GME funds. The program would support new residency slots in primary care or other high need specialties, not supported by GME payments, in teaching hospitals and other community-based health care facilities with a focus on ambulatory and preventive care, value, and reducing health system costs over the long-term. Funds will be targeted to training programs that feature concepts such as team-based care, the effective incorporation of health information technology into clinical practice, population health, and telemedicine. Special consideration will be given to rural areas. It is expected that this program will produce 13,000 physicians over the next ten years. Two current HRSA programs will be supported by this new mandatory funding: the Children's Hospital Graduate Medical Education Program[10] and the Teaching Health Center Program[11].

> Modernizing Graduate Medical Education: The new HRSA grant program, Targeted Support for Graduate Medical Education, proposed in the 2015 budget request, builds on the ACA GME provisions, will train 13,000 new residents in primary care and high need specialties, and is an important first step in better shaping graduate medical education to align with national needs.

This program will expand the reach of other HRSA workforce training programs funded by Titles VII and VIII of the Public Health Service Act. These programs represent what have been the Department's largest discretionary investments in workforce training. Several of these programs received funding from ARRA[12]. Many of these programs were reauthorized by the ACA and additional funding was provided in 2010 with funding from the ACA's Prevention and Public Health Fund. Awards were made in 2010 for a five year initiative, with new support for training primary care residents ($198 million), nurse practitioners ($31 million), and physician assistants ($30 million). These investments are training 1,700 new primary care providers.

Additional awards were made in 2012 for a three-year initiative to train 200 additional mental and behavioral health practitioners.

C. Loan and Scholarship Programs

Key to the Department's efforts to address the uneven distribution of health care professionals across the nation is the National Health Service Corps (NHSC). Founded in 1972, the NHSC is the Department's largest program of obligated scholarships and loans. The NHSC has provided scholarships and loan repayment to physicians, advanced practice nurses, physician assistants, dentists and certain other providers, including behavioral health providers, in return for practice in a designated HPSA. The American Recovery and Reinvestment Act revitalized the NHSC through a $300 million short-term infusion in 2009 through 2011. This funding was more than double the NHSC's appropriation for 2009. The ACA built on this base, providing approximately $1.5 billion for 2011 through 2015 for the NHSC. Enhanced funding for the NHSC allowed its field strength to more than double from 3,600 in 2008 to nearly 8,900 by the end of Fiscal Year 2013. These providers are currently caring for approximately 9.3 million people in all 50 states. Roughly half of all NHSC providers meet their service obligation at federally-funded health centers. About 45 percent of all NHSC providers serve in rural sites; in 26 states there are more rural NHSC providers than urban. A pilot program, begun in 2011, expands eligibility for NHSC providers to Critical Access Hospitals affiliated with an outpatient ambulatory clinic. Retention in the NHSC is high. Approximately 85 percent of NHSC participants continue to provide care to the underserved up to two years after their obligation is completed while 55 percent continue to provide care to the underserved ten years after having completed their obligations; the default rate is less than 1 percent[13].

The need for NHSC providers remains high across the country with demand exceeding current funding levels. Funding priority is given to clinicians working at NHSC sites in communities designated as high need. The Department's decision to seek substantial new funding for the NHSC is built on the longstanding needs of underserved rural and inner city areas, the NHSC's proven retention record, and continued demands for primary and other health care services.

National Health Service Corps: The President's budget proposes a sustained level of commitment to the NHSC through 2020 totaling $3.95 billion. The President's proposal will allow the program to grow to support 15,000 providers per year and also give the Secretary the flexibility to expand NHSC eligibility to other high-need disciplines and service sites on a temporary basis.

D. Promotion of Quality and Efficiency through Delivery System Reform

Key components of ARRA laid some of the groundwork for improving the efficiency and quality of health care delivery. One of its components was the Health Information Technology for Economic and Clinical Health (HITECH) Act, a part of ARRA, which set forth an ambitious program for building health information technology (HIT) into the delivery system. The interconnected employment of incentives and penalties related to meaningful use of electronic health records (EHRs) is intended to make care delivery more efficient and to give providers new tools to improve both individual and population health. This has resulted in a rapid increase in adoption of HIT, with more than 60 percent of eligible physicians (and other professionals) and 85 percent of eligible hospitals receiving incentive payments for adopting and using EHRs.

Health centers, funded by HRSA, are playing a critical role in system redesign because they provide accessible and dependable sources of primary care services in underserved communities. The ACA established the Community Health Center Fund that is providing $11 billion over five years for the operation, expansion, and construction of health centers across the country. The nation's 1,200 health centers operate 9,200 delivery sites and, in 2012, provided care to 21.1 million people. Health centers emphasize coordinated primary and preventive services for low-income individuals, racial and ethnic minorities, rural communities, and other underserved populations. They place emphasis on the coordination and comprehensiveness of care, the ability to manage patients with multiple health care needs, and the use of key quality improvement practices, including health information technology. The health center model also embraces a team-based approach to care that includes physicians, nurse practitioners, physician assistants, nurses, dental providers, midwives, behavioral health care providers, social workers, health educators, and many others. Team-based models allow providers to leverage the knowledge and skills of all team members, including allowing those with higher levels of training to focus on more complex cases and all to practice to the full extent of their licenses.

In November 2010, HRSA established a patient-centered medical home initiative to promote more effective and efficient care in health centers. To date, more than 40 percent of health centers have been recognized. Health centers also reduce costs to health systems; the health center model of care has been shown to reduce the use of costlier providers of care, such as emergency departments and hospitals.

But perhaps the greatest promise for health system redesign comes through the previously discussed service delivery and payment reform models of the Innovation Center. Established by the ACA, the Innovation Center is funding a growing portfolio of project models all directed at improving care delivery and/or reducing costs. Models that reduce spending without reducing the quality of care or improve the quality of care without increasing costs can be expanded and disseminated so that best practices can be adopted more broadly.

Virtually every Innovation Center demonstration has workforce implications: For example: the Innovation Center, in partnership with HRSA and building on HRSA efforts, has engaged 473 Federally Qualified Health Center (FQHC) sites to participate in a FQHC Advanced Primary Care Demonstration to test the effectiveness of doctors and other health professionals working in teams to coordinate and improve care for Medicare patients. Participating FQHCs are expected to achieve Level 3 patient-centered medical home recognition, help patients manage chronic conditions, as well as actively coordinate care for patients.

However, one set of Innovation Center projects has particular workforce relevance. In 2012, about $1 billion was awarded to 107 grantees across the country in the first round of Health Care Innovation Awards. These projects needed to address the Innovation Center's broad themes of better, more cost effective care, but in addition applicants were required to address workforce implications of their projects. Awarded projects varied in design. Many proposed new staffing arrangements. Primary care proposals frequently emphasized the medical team and expanded use of employees such as community health workers. A second round of applications is under review.

The Department is confident that it can learn from these projects to further inform how care should be delivered, how it should be paid for, how medical teams can function more effectively, the skill sets providers need today and in the future, and how the Department can deploy its resources more effectively in its workforce training programs.

V. Conclusion

The Administration, led by the Department, has been focused on ensuring that the nation's health care workforce is properly prepared and deployed to meet the needs of the 21st century. The Department has developed a workforce vision that is guided by the principles that we must move toward a value-based delivery system, improve access to primary care, make full use of every member of the health team, align workforce to population needs, and use workforce levers to transform health care delivery. The Department has a number of available policy levers. By using these, developing and employing appropriate performance measures, and working through its agencies, it can continue to focus on creating and supporting a cadre of highly trained health care providers who are well-distributed and prepared to serve in an evolving health care delivery system. The new proposals in the President's FY 2015 budget are a major step in advancing these objectives.

End Notes

[1] See for example, FACT SHEET: Creating Jobs by Addressing Primary Care Workforce Needs; http://www.hhs.gov/healthcare/facts/factsheets/2013/06/jobs06212012.html.

[2] Based on the Federal Government's Standard Occupational Classification system of identifying workforce categories.

[3] The U.S. Health Workforce Chartbook – In Brief HRSA/National Center for Health Workforce Analysis November 2013 http://bhpr.hrsa.gov/healthworkforce/supplydemand/usworkforce/chartbook/index.html.

[4] In geographic HPSAs, PCIP qualifying physicians receive both bonuses.

[5] http://kff.org/medicaid/issue-brief/how-much-will-medicaid-physician-fees-for/.

[6] See: Medicaid Graduate Medical Education Payments; A Fifty State Survey https://members.aamc.org/eweb/upload/Medicaid%20Graduate%20Medical%20Education%20Payments%20A%2050-State%20Survey.pdf.

[7] See: Health Affairs: The Geography of Graduate Medical Education: Imbalances Signal Need for New Distribution Policies; Fitzhugh Mullan, Candice Chen and Erika Steinmetz; Health Affairs, 32, no.11, (2013): 1014-1921.

[8] Among family practice physicians, for example, 56 percent of graduates practice within 100 miles of residency training. See: Graham Center Policy One-Pager "Migration After Family Medicine Residency: 56% of Graduates Practice Within 100 Miles of Training" E. Blake

Fagan; Sean C. Finnegan; Andrew W. Bazemore; Claire B. Gibbons; and Stephen M. Petterson; www.graham-center.org/online/etc/media.

[9] http://www.medpac.gov/chapters/jun10_ch04.pdf.

[10] Because Medicare GME is tied to Medicare payment, payments to pediatric teaching hospitals historically were limited. To address this point, in 1999, Congress enacted the Children's Hospital GME program. This program provides a payment to free standing children's hospitals that is modeled after Medicare's direct and indirect GME payments. Currently about 55 children's hospitals receive these payments. The 2014 appropriation is $265 million.

[11] In order to encourage primary care training in community settings, the ACA established the Teaching Health Center GME program, operated by HRSA, to give opportunities for residency training in the ambulatory settings in which primary care physicians and dentists practice. Funded with up to $230 million, to date more than 40 residency programs are providing training for nearly 350 residents. Close to half the training sites are located in medically underserved communities and/or health professions shortage areas.

[12] ARRA provided $200 million for HRSA's Title VII and Title VIII workforce programs.

[13] There are also similar loan and scholarship programs directed at Native Americans and Native Hawaiians. A recent NHSC focus has been increasing placements at Indian Health Service and tribal sites.

INDEX

A

B

C

D

N

O

P

Q

R

S

T

U

V

W